BEYOND DISCOURAGEMENT

## CREATIVITY

# BEYOND DISCOURAGEMENT
# CREATIVITY

An essay on the raising of a creative child

Bernard Aimé Poulin

A Classic Perceptions Publication

Cover design by: Bernard A. Poulin

Copyright © 2010 by Bernard Aimé Poulin

ISBN: 978-0-9866803-0-4

The author and the publisher disclaim all liability as to the use of the information contained in this book. The contents are provided as information only.

All rights reserved. No part of this book may be reproduced, stored, or transmitted by any means – whether auditory, graphic, mechanical, or electronic – without written permission of both publisher and author, except in the case of brief excerpts used in critical articles and reviews. Unauthorized reproduction of any part of this work is illegal and is punishable by law.

*Unless otherwise noted, quotes interspersed throughout the book in italics are attributable to the author. The year these comments were made (or appeared in a conference, article or lecture) is indicated.*

# Acknowledgements

Many thanks go to:

In 1988, Johanna Lamourie-Tiffin (aka Ainsley's mom) was fascinated by an article in a small art newspaper. The title of the piece was: *How To Raise A Creative Child*. When she later had a daughter of her own, she remembered the article and appreciated having read it. Nearly 25 years later, Johanna and I met for the first time. She suggested I should "elaborate on the original article". This book is the result of that chance encounter.

I also sincerely thank:

Ron Ensom, M.S.W, RSW and Mary Elizabeth Picher, M.A.for their expert reviews and personal comments.

And last but definitely not least, I recognize:

Philip Street. His superbly rendered cartoon strip "Fisher" appears daily in Canada's Globe and Mail newspaper. To this wondrously gifted cartoonist, animator and illustrator I humbly say thanks for the 2 pertinent strips he allowed to be used in this book. For more of his insightful and humorous creations, regarding contemporary family life and child-rearing, check out his work at www.fisher.com.

*If I was half as curious as my cat Laurier, I would be a thousand times more creative. - 02*

# Dedication

With all of my heart I dedicate this book
to Marie
the most precious friend, extraordinary love and most wondrous
wife any man could hope to have.

And how could this book not be dedicated to her? . . .
She is, very much, the most creative person I know.

XXX moi

# Preamble

In the visual arts, a sketch or preliminary drawing provides a basis upon which an idea is further elaborated. Sketching allows for a disciplined yet free-form expression of a concept. And in this, sketching is akin to an "essay", a composition based on an informed yet subjective review and evaluation of time, place, context, and their inherent conundrums.

*Beyond discouragement - Creativity* is therefore a sketch. It is not written by someone who professes to be a sociologist, self-help guru or pop-psychology mentor. I am a painter - a visual artist fascinated by the world around me. I observe for a living. Wondering is what I do as I daily encounter the uniqueness of individuals who inhabit our globe and cause it to be what it is and aspires to be.

By extension, I am also passionate about creativity and its encouragement. Upset by the seemingly generalized practice of discouragement in our society - and being constantly wary of the individuals and groups who profit from making as many of us so - I began studying the discouragement phenomenon. I wanted to know what causes us to abandon our "selves" to the control of others.

In light of this, my first reflections and observations were laid down nearly 40 years ago. As such, the following pages are simply a review of these "wonderings".

Being an optimist, my only hope is that these pages will raise questions and even shackles, cause discussions to happen, passions to be stirred and the encouragement of creativity to become prevalent in the daily lives of every child on the face of our planet.

Thank you for taking the time to read and to wonder too.

*Sincerely, Bernard Poulin*

Fascination - Graphite & C Pencil - 1988

# Contents

Preamble v

Introduction 1

1  The Conundrum 5

2  The Context 61

3  The Key 109

Bibliography 190

Biography 192

*Life is neither incredibly wonderful nor incredibly horrible. More often than not, it is simply horribly and wonderfully incredible - 81*

# Introduction

In 1988, based on several years of observations of families, schools and our North American environment, I wrote an article entitled: How To Raise A Creative Child. In it, I simply offered parents uncomplicated preventives and suggestions. Actually, my whole reasoning was based on a series of wants. . . I wanted parents to become parents again - to be more than simply providers of goods, shelter and food to their children. I wanted children to regain the power of creativity, to reconnect with the significant adults in their lives. I wanted children to feel the joy of life, the hope for a future worthy of their aspirations and efforts. I wanted them to get a taste of a world in which they would not only strive to be the best they can be - but dare to be even better than their own expectations. Encouraged by a reader of that first article on creative parenting, I have completed this book. Not a lighthearted piece, it highlights how important encouragement and creativity really are to our children's and the world's survival - especially now. . . now that we live in an environment which increasingly seems focussed on the destruction of individual uniqueness and creativity.

The first 2 chapters present a review of the problems we face every day and the negative aspects of the environment which nurture those problems. But in the last chapter, I focus on reversing the power of a negative environment even though that may require a dogged determination and a revised philosophy of encouragement.

Is it doable? Absolutely. In my estimation, the health of our children and the future of us all are in the balance.

In essence, we have to stop thinking that every problem, as complicated as it might seem, needs an equally complex solution. We have to stop believing that nothing can be realised without the expenditure of huge sums or the purportedly sage advice of self-anointed authority figures of the day. Pop-psychology specialists and the ever domineering and manipulative marketplace do not have the answer we are looking for. Even less, are healthy alternatives available to us through the surreptitious "lurings" of pharmaceutical enterprises and those who would have us believe that every purported symptom or syndrome is in need of a quick (read: chemical) fix.

In the last chapter I basically outline the same information I offered parents decades ago. These are plain, unadulterated, uncomplicated and generic offerings. Their purpose is to stimulate more specific activities and ideas which can only be personalized by the significant adults in a child's life. Each parent knows their own child. They know what makes them "tick", what turns their head, excites their interests, goads them to be adventurous or animated.

I suggest jotting down ideas on the margins of the book's pages. The more we add to our creativity arsenal, the more ideas we get. There is nothing more exciting than to watch a child blossom and grow to ever greater heights based on the encouragement we offer. I would be most proud to discover one of my books in a second hand bin all scribbled with plans, suggestions, comments and ideas! What a tribute that would be to the parents and children who grew up on those encouraging footnotes.

For all intents and purposes I believe that all communities, at one time or another, thrive and at other times suffer. And when a community, society or nation suffers, the only way it can right itself - become whole again - is if every individual member chooses to take a first step in the process of healing. This is especially so when the only help being offered us is one which seems determined to render us all homogeneously submissive to its dictates and beneficent attentions. . . So my ideas are simple. . . Let's show our kids we love them more than life itself. Let's encourage them to be more than they believe they can be. Creativity is what took us from the cave to the moon and on to ever greater heights. It is only through that same concept of individual creativity that our societies and countries will regain their collective pride and progress.

*Bernard Poulin*

# 1
## The Conundrum

Saturday Night - Graphite – 1984

*When the infinite vastness of a child's creativity is realized, one can only weep at the loss of childhood. - 91*

## The Birth of Creativity

Childhood creativity knows no bounds. Physiologically and psychologically, infants are programmed to grow. Motivation is unnecessary to a healthy child. From birth, the heart and soul are ready for action. Reoccurring amazement feeds an insatiable curiosity. Wondrous close-at-hand sensations which the eye can see, the fingers grasp, the ears hear and the nose detect are the first teasers - luring imagination and discovery to the fore. Eventually though, the fog of distance lifts. Reaching beyond initial close-up sensations is suddenly possible. And with that, a new and ever more exciting reality unfolds.

Over time, all infants integrate all of these sensations. They become more and more a part of who the children are. And yet, what is most incredible in the beginning life of all human infants is that at this point they have yet to encounter the greatest of their budding discoveries. As dramatic as their lives have been up to now, yet another sudden and intense seminal moment will occur. And when it does, it will be a shocking split second happening - one whose impact will last the rest of each child's life. . .

> *One day, it becomes crystal clear that this new and exciting realm they have entered is not just made up of "them" but rather is an extension of - and then a "something" beyond themselves.*

And so, through their ever-increasing observations, primal analyses and tingling eureka moments, all of these accumulating sensual discoveries begin to "make sense" - as much as infants can fathom the concept of analytical sense. And as a child's excitement mounts so do its daily forays into this incredible world. For it is upon this self-motivated energy and a creative impulse that healthy growth and survival depends.

# BEYOND DISCOURAGEMENT – CREATIVITY

Now, if it is true that the root elements of *creativity* are innate - if it is, somehow, through the senses deeply linked to and entrenched in the human psyche... what does this say about each of us? what does this say about our "being-ness" - about our capacity to move forward, to move beyond our "selves", to imprint our unique creative mark upon a world filled with unique "others"? Despite all of the scientific research and speculation of the past centuries, these questions have never fully been answered.

Nonetheless, what we do know is that from the first deeply inhaled and exhaled breath of a newborn, talents and abilities begin to unfold - and this, mostly through infant volition. Every new day brings on more and more findings, spurred on by the environment's tastes, smells, sensations and sounds. And how these are later enacted upon is defined by how they affect "that" particular human being's perceptions. And how that unique person interprets sensations determines the "who" and "what" of their specific evolving self. For all intents and purposes, the arrival of each new child is "the" most awesome representation of what miraculous evolution truly is.

## Stimulus?

Children need nothing more to grow and thrive than to be faced with what is. Stimulus, to a child, is simply life laying itself before it - wishing itself upon this new being in order that it discover all of its mysteries. And so it is, that at the very root of the concept of individual creativity, within a collective environment, lies the simplest and yet most complex enticement: *encouragement*.

And even though children need little else but space and freedom, that encouragement must be there if a child is to thrive and give. Nothing stems from or grows within an environmental vacuum. Plants require air, water and nutrients. They feed the environment from which a positive pattern of growth can be established. Now, air, water and nutrients don't force or push a plant to grow. They are simply there, available and richly encouraging to the growing plant which seems to know to "take them in". How this occurs in each individual plant determines the unique impact that, in turn, each plant will have on its environment. This analogy can easily be applied to human creativity - but with one crucial element being substantially emphasized.

## The "Other"

To the human soul, environment is not simply water, air and nutrients. In human terms, one key factor can readily lay claim to the exercise of power over the intensity with which creativity either flourishes, or not, in an individual.

We are all born into a world of never-ending, tingling "connections" - simply put: a world where bees need plants and plants need bees in order that both can be the best they can be. Without this simple concept regarding a complex world, life as we know it cannot exist. We humans are part of this whole process. But, we cannot be or do anything without acknowledging that our world is richly populated by an alluring and mysterious element known as "others". If truth be told, the main goal of "others" is the very distraction of the self from the self - from the aloneness (solitude) required by the creative impulse. At its best, this element plays a major role in providing an encouraging atmosphere which allows creativity to flower. In essence, the concept of the "other" is either a catalyst for balance or the lack of it in our lives. For at its worst, an "other" can also destroy or seriously curtail creative expression.

At first glance, an infant is unaware of this "otherness". In the beginning, "other" appears as simply one more detail in the total package that attracts and stimulates the senses. But gradually, this additional element in the life of the evolving infant causes one of the most sophisticated of eureka moments to occur in the human brain.

When the minds of children primitively formulate the intriguing concept of "otherness", an exciting and powerful new dimension enters their being. The very presence of this "other", causes a mysterious yet immeasurable pleasure to occur. With time, this other becomes even more alluring than a child's initial single-minded quest for discoveries and adventures. And so this find, this intense presence of an "other", evolves into what can only be called a "connection" - a symbiotic link which alters the primary activities of self-expression first enacted by the child. And the combination of the now "two separate others" eventually creates a bond which, in effect, impacts forever on anything and everything the child will encounter and do or not do in the future.

## Connecting

Early on, a child's first grasp of connection is one-sided. It is entranced by the feeling of being recognized - (as in: being the centre of the universe). But eventually the subconscious recognition of the other as an "actual" other evolves - the otherness becoming more and more "real". Eventually, being accepted, nurtured and loved by this other (as much as love can be understood at this stage) become powerful driving forces. Simply being recognized is no longer enough. And the older a child gets, the more excited it becomes as "the other" multiplies itself into an environment of "others". And, as time passes, the number of significant connections increases and the need and want to also be accepted by them grows exponentially. Nonetheless, some of these multiple connections gel more deeply than others - creating an intimate conspiracy which has some "others" intensely involved and some less so in the life of the growing child. And because there is a loss of some others and a retention of closeness with especial others, a new sensation arises. And this feeling dictates a need to "not" displease - to not take chances on losing the attentions and services of the closer "significant others".

Now this intense human bonding does exact a price - a blow to the neutral state of a newborn's self-stimulating environment - its arena of creativity - its total "me" existence. As a newly bonded creature, an infant's elemental sensuous nature is forced, therefore, to evolve - to sublimate its urges, to submit to this new and vital discovery of connectedness.

This is not to say that children completely abandon their interest in self-stimulating creative activities. But what it does mean is that when the environment in which children find themselves expands, it also becomes more complex. And when that happens, defining and satisfying needs and wants must be constantly revised. To be both members of an ever-enlarging society and to also strive to be unique is a struggle - a constant challenge which must be dealt with. To keep up, children must learn to cope - to select, to deal with and to decide what is important and what is not. In essence, they must choose what is or is not essential to "their" particular basic survival requirements.

From the moment a child is born, the amount of learning which must occur, the amount of information which must be assimilated is extraordinary. That it all happens to a small child whose analytical capacities are far from being thorough is amazing in and of itself. But the fact that most children survive their first 5 years emotionally and mentally intact - is actually even more incredible. For, in the area of family communications alone, multiple personalities constantly vie for each other's attention. While defining their own person from within a clan, small children face a varied array of communication styles, needs, wants and multi-directional family dynamic parameters. In simpler terms:

"It ain't easy being a kid!"

## Family Dynamics And Intimacy

When intimate connections are being formed within a very limited geographic space - such as a home environment - tensions can and do occur. But children are quick studies. They soon learn that dealing with the cultural and or social "impositions" of that environment is a priority. These impositions, commonly referred to as *socially acceptable behaviours and norms*, begin to shape the young individual's coping skills.

Despite this situation - and in part because of it - a child's primary instincts "will themselves" to survive. Children learn quickly what their base requirements are - i.e: to maintain emotional stability by 1-not causing the loss of key connections with the most important "others" in their lives and 2- creating a balance of give and take - i.e. not over-testing key connections with those who, "like" them, are children BUT. . . They are older, wiser and bigger. . . Whether we like it or not, the very idea of knowing who the "top dog" is does play a major role in the socialization of us all.

But once these parameters become ingrained, and if they are consistent. . . children soon feel secure enough to once again take on the defining of who they individually are. And so, seeing to the requirements of both of these essentials (i.e. social integrity and personal definition) is crucial - and therein lies the importance of the concept of supporting and encouraging and feeling supported and encouraged.

It therefore follows that the roles played by significant adults are crucial. Parents, teachers and mentors provide balance. Adults have been through childhood. They have survived it - or not. Possibly they were encouraged as children. Possibly they were not. But regardless of the quality of their own upbringing, reality dictates that having a child to care for becomes the main "natural" focus in an adult's life - not their missed or "mythed" childhood.

As such, significant adults are responsible for providing the very environment in which a child must strike out in order to become the best they can be. And for some lucky children, this is the opportunity to go even further - i.e. to go beyond their own personal best. And for encouraged children this means being and becoming increasingly themselves rather than stagnating as undefined clones of their significant adult others.

Now, having had a difficult childhood may handicap an individual playing the role of significant adult, but that past should not be the essential determinant which defines the value of a parent, teacher or mentor's capacity to provide a nurturing environment. Most parents care deeply, despite their personal handicaps. And most parents, despite personal past or present pains, give the best they can to the children they have. In essence, good parenting is not the domain of those who purportedly had "perfect" childhoods. Neither is it the realm of those who follow the latest trends, as laid out by pocket-book specialists. Parenting is available to all who wish it - not because of honed or cloned perfection and not because of pain - but rather despite one, the other or both.

## The Discouragement of Perfection

Thankfully, perfection is not a state often sought by many. That's because it is, in actual fact, the preserve of saints and angels. No human has ever reached such a lofty position. And none but the arrogant try. I say thankfully because those who seek perfection are more often than not the same individuals who impose it upon the rest of us who are simply trying to do the best we can.

We are the significant adults in our children's lives. Our role is not to be saintly. Rather, our quest is to show children how to be human - i.e. wondrously imperfect. Our role is to be the best our knowledge base allows us to be. This is where *excellence* comes in. Excellence is flexible enough to be achievable. It allows room for error and failure. It says that today I can try to do the best I can with the proviso that tomorrow I can strive to do and be even better - (that is, if some idiot doesn't discourage me from trying.)

> *Excellence can never be achieved when societies formulate and impose standards based on perfectionist dictates - or worse, evaluate and judge through a lowest common denominator lens of political correctness. - 01*

Now, North Americans come from great stock. Some of our ancestors were already on the continent. Others came to these shores willingly and others not so willingly. Regardless, the advantages we enjoy today were hewn through the toil and muscle, trial and error and pains of each of these brave souls.

Some arrived well-heeled, others without a *sou. But, as has been proven over and over by many generations of immigrants, refugees, one room school houses and poverty-stricken areas of our nations' big and small cities - a parent does not have to be schooled, rich, genius, middle-class or even speak the same language as their child.

> \* *"sou" (pronounced: sue) - a former French coin of low denomination*

What caring parents do have in common is the determination to encourage their children to go forward and onward. As long as the goal is to do well by their children, such parents can consider their job not only well done but done admirably.

*Have no fear of perfection, you'll never reach it. - Dali*

Let's face it, our children are not the ones demanding that we be perfect, wealthy, handsome, educated or erudite. What children want is love from those they hold dear. They simply want recognition and encouragement in order to become strong, and more independent as children, adolescents and adults. Children demand no more than this and deserve no less than that. In light of the above, please permit me a revealing aside: Many years ago, as a young wanna-be artist, I was unable to afford professional models. I therefore spent many hours in city parks, observing and sketching people of all ages. My subjects were mainly picnicking families. Elders played board games and ambled slowly about, smiling or scowling at children, boisterously trying to outdo each other. Parents sipped wine or guzzled beer while teasing each other and arguing about sports or political affiliations.

During these sessions, limitless expressions of varied emotions played themselves out before me. I saw all types of family constellations and dynamics. But despite some evident communication problems (which today would easily be defined as nefarious) I came away with one obvious fact: children love their parents more

# BEYOND DISCOURAGEMENT – CREATIVITY

unconditionally than the other way around. And over the years that hasn't changed much at all.

In 1972, I even recorded in my sketchbook a rather awkward poem. (One which highlights my obvious lack of genius in the area of poetry.) Nonetheless, the scribbled sentiments do pay tribute to love at its most pure.

*Fat is nothing*
*When loved by a child.*
*Thin is abstract... and*
*So are warts, jowls and cataracts.*
*Big noses or rimmed glasses,*
*Bowed legs or knobby knees,*
*Chewed nails or stringy hair,*
*Tired eyes or buck teeth,*
*Freckles and/or callouses - all for nought...*
*Stubbly beard or holey socks,*
*A coat of cotton or of fur,*
*Whether called ma'm or sir,*
*The smell of sweat or of sleep,*
*The essence of "Brute" or "Irish Spring",*
*By a child... No less loved are you.*
*Whether beautiful or plain,*
*Handsome or insane, young or old,*
*A child sees none of these.*
*Your dress or looks make not your fame.*
*A child pays no cost and asks no fee.*
*A child simply loves... for free. - 72*

No child has ever wished for perfection in the significant adults in their lives. All children ever want is a positive environment - an atmosphere conducive to not only continued growth but most especially to continued adventurous discoveries. And this *encouragement* is the very key upon which their future depends. Encouragement is what allows a child not only to survive but to stretch, to create and to go above and beyond even their own expectations. Creative action is what elevates a child from a plateau of dependency to a mountain range of "eventual adult" control of its own destiny. To encourage this is to offer the greatest of parental, teaching or mentoring gifts.

King Of The Mountain - Oil - 9" x 7"

## Caveat

But even though such a gift is undeniably the most important offering we can make to our children - it doesn't seem to register in our 21$^{st}$ century psyche. It even seems to frighten us.

Despite the riches of our times, and possibly because of them, affection, parenting, support and encouragement have been redefined. And these re-definitions are rooted in terms which discourage creativity. More and more we relegate our significant adult roles to programmed rather than natural connections with our children - programmed connections as laid out by specialists - specialists in both behavioural and promotional fields. Advertising now determines which market-based stimuli, electronic gadgets and teaching tools are considered appropriate for our children while pocket-book gurus (rather than cultural value systems) determine whether our attitudes are fit (or not) for the parenting arena.

The proliferation of professionally designed, so-called educational toys, stimulus games and adult-directed activities are not signs, despite what we are told, that we are more loving or caring. (That we have to be convinced of this is bizarre to say the least!) Rather, they are signs of how inadequate we feel and how much wider the gulf is between children and parents than it has been in the past 100 years. And if the excessive number of "play paraphernalia" in many households is any indication - that disconnect is rather more a Grand Canyon than a gully.

Though difficult to fathom, the forces of the market place have become the supervisors of and mentors to our children. By the age of 3 a child is even considered a worthy member of a "demographic" by marketers. Their voices, minds and hearts are worth every penny of the more than 2 billion dollars spent on them annually in advertising.

But how can the marketplace purport to hold dear the well-being of our children? And even more importantly, how is it that we allow them to? The primary purpose of any business enterprise is the profit margin. But everyday we are manipulated into believing that our children will not get a proper education or be prepared for the future unless they reap the benefits of specific products created by "concerned" manufacturers. In essence, the marketplace has usurped the major aspect of our significant adult roles. Surreptitiously, "it" has become the knowing and caring "parent". We, on the other hand, have been relegated to the lesser "worker-ant" position of: "provider".

The marketplace tells us that to meet the standards and demands of tomorrow's world our children must have the highest high-tech school equipment, the most advanced (read: ever-changing) teaching techniques along with the accompanying new and improved educational materials and text books. Nonetheless, no one seems to acknowledge that despite these "advanced" materials and environments our North American children (when compared with the rest of the world) are not doing as well as anticipated in math, sciences or languages - i.e. in the areas of necessary survival skills.

In the past 50 years, we have come to believe that the only way to meet "children's needs" is to provide them with the most expensive and expansive equipment and facilities which take away not only their natural passion for learning but actually take all the fun out of "overcoming difficulties". But most especially, these "easy solution tools" drastically curb children from daring - i.e. from stretching themselves further and further - a technique children naturally use to excitedly place the bar of achievement ever higher for themselves.

But with a contemporary parental need to hover and to overprotect and a demanding more of and, at the same time, a demanding less of our children - an atmosphere of total confusion

# BEYOND DISCOURAGEMENT – CREATIVITY

and bewilderment arises in their hearts and minds. Rather than offer activities and implement programs which actually do challenge our children, we weaken them by making a portion of their lives completely perplexing and another portion so comfortable they are bored. And to children, programmed boredom is nothing less than discouraging. In essence, children realise early on that what is being offered them has nothing to do with them at all.

Now children, more bored than encouraged, automatically spend increasing amounts of time mesmerized by monitors and television screens. With imagination stifled by programmed toys and games which determine what is or is not play, what is or is not "educational", there is really nothing left for a child to do but become idle - with a penchant for regurgitation of what is considered "acceptable". When this happens, children become robotically adept at advising their "providers" as to which sugar or sodium laden foods they should ingest in order to "grow up to be big and strong" and what name-brands are needed to fulfill their exaggerated (when not "entitled") self-esteem requirements.

And like television sound bytes gone mad they spew the contents of memorized ads, reminding us which up-to-date equipment and educational toys they require and which name-brand electronic paraphernalia they must have in order to be accepted by their peers. And do some parents take these "suggestions" into account when spending their hard-earned cash? Yes, many of "us" do...

That submissive parental attitudes are one of the root causes of the problems faced by today's children doesn't seem to register. .. even when the health of those children is in jeopardy. Salt, sugar, preservatives - unhealthy alternatives to required nutrients, coupled with an excessively sedentary lifestyle, have become part and parcel of who we all are. And so, no one really questions the inherent dangers we daily impose upon ourselves and our children. They're all just accepted as "normal" things we encounter everyday.

Despite the fact that Canadians and Americans are creating more and more obese offspring then ever before, those self-same children are more appearance obsessed than any generation since the beginning of time. But none of this seems to phase anybody - whether adult or child. Recently (early in the year of 2010), a large scale study of 4 to 12 years olds was conducted by an eastern Ontario cardiovascular disease prevention network. Their findings are the following:

- 90% of parents believe their children are active enough. The reality is that 87% of children fail to exercise adequately.

- 75% of parents believe their children spend no more than 2 hours a day in front of a television or computer. The reality is that only 10% of children spend less than 2 hours a day before a television or computer screen.

- 60% of parents believe their children eat enough fruit and vegetables. In reality, only 12% of children eat enough fruit and vegetables.

- 63% of parents think their children drink no more than 3 soft drinks a week. The reality? 33% of children have at least one soft drink every day.

- Parental perception on obesity? 83% of parents believe their children do not have a weight problem. 76% are not at all preoccupied by their children's obvious weight problems. But reality dictates that 28% of children between 2 and 17 are either overweight or obese.

Because the overall contemporary environment seems to be wearing blinders, it is not surprising that children, from a very young age, display signs of early onset cholesterol, heart and diabetes related symptoms. That there is no outrage over this situation is what flabbergasts the most.

Add to this conundrum an increasing equal and opposite reaction to body image which extols the virtues of total thinness and what we have is increasing psychological and physical distress at both ends of the body-image spectrum.

When children, as young as those in their pre-teen years, look into a mirror and react with disappointment and even self-loathing, someone out there has to begin to take notice.

## Over-fed and Under-nourished

We live in bizarre times. How have our separate countries gone from being nations of builders and creative genius to societies of improperly educated children and adolescents who, increasingly, and after only a short 10 minute walk breathe so heavily they need a 20 minute rest? And worse, when they find themselves at rest they have no idea what to do with themselves without their technical gadgetry in hand. How are they to take the helm of our communities in the not so distant future if self-control, imagination and reasonable decision-making powers are not part of their make-up? How have we gone from supporting incredibly creative small community school organizations which helped build a world-renowned democratic system, to "letting" the powers that be turn these into massive, cold and impersonal academic factories to which we mindlessly send our over-fed and under-nourished children everyday?

We seem hell-bent on producing less functional children and less independent adolescents. Why? Our children are now being "processed" in industry-like facilities which house more children per square foot than some of our discouragingly numerous and even more punitive, and therefore dysfunctional, penal institutions?

The question is not do we go back to the old one-room school house? The questions are: How do we get the same success and creative values from our present dysfunctional systems that were available to children in leaner and meaner times? Do we rid ourselves of these systems and start over again? Do we stop, drop and roll in order to strangle the flames of apathy which seem to be consuming us whole? How do we incorporate contemporary benefits and materials into our educational systems in such a way as to not stifle creative potential? How do we keep our children healthy enough, long enough, to grow into the prosperous adults we purportedly wish them to become?

Naturally, one family unit cannot be imposed upon to feel responsible for the woes of the world. BUT, every parent needs to feel responsible and privileged to be a mentor to their own child. Every parent needs to feel deep down in their gut that the environment, whose role it is to nurture, must be the best that it can be. And if it is not, why not? And lastly, who and what is responsible and how can this problem be faced and fixed?

But adults beware. . . solutions to our dilemmas will rarely be found in the manipulated responses we've been fed these past many years. Rather, they can probably be found within the questions we never seem to ask.

## When The Best Isn't Our Best

But isn't giving our children the best that we give them the same as giving them what's best? Sadly, no. . .

What we now consider "best" has, over the past century, been dictated to us by those who profit from saying that it is. And these same entities need to have us believe that their products "are" the best that "we" can offer our children.

But then, we really aren't offering anything to them when the determination of what is good for our children is established, not by us, but by those who are selling us the recommended product. Children do not succeed and never will succeed in life when their futures are in the hands of materials or entities which have nothing to do with nurturing creativity, and even less to do with individual thinking or the stimulation of an imagination.

Again, part of the conundrum is that we are no longer perceived as parents - as responsible guides and mentors. Our roles have been eroded. We are not who we think we are. Rather, and more simply, we have been designated "providers" - those who pay for what is deemed to be (by the powers that be) a "requirement" of a healthy contemporary life. We are no longer judge of what is good for our children. Specialists and advertisers act in that capacity. And they can because they have assured us that we can't - that we don't know how to - and that we are in need of support in this "oh so specialized area" that is child rearing. We are, therefore, simply enablers. We pay the fees. In turn, the children have their role to play - they pay the consequences.

BERNARD POULIN

## To Be Or Not To Be

There is an additional problem involved with our present system which eventually, yet surreptitiously, leads our children down the garden path. Today's "manufactured" education, educational materials and programmed activity toys consistently promote the concept of "easy". Easy eliminates "difficult" and difficult is not what we want in our "fun", "young" and "TGIF" societies, is it? Making everything easy (and equating easy as an absolute requirement of fun) teaches a child that growing up, today, is an opportunity *to not do* anything that is remotely related to the idea of work or the expending of effort or energy.

Today, adults adhere to a concept of not forcing children to submit to anything that is demanding of them, bothers them, annoys them or upsets them. Ironically, this tactic renders our children weak - incapable of handling failure or difficulties of any kind. And because they are not made to face and deal, they eventually find themselves submitting to the demands, directions, exhortations and manipulations of others.

To not have to cope, deal with or truly accomplish sells the idea that it's OK to "take it easy", to be more childish, to not grow up, to not try, to not work. Life is the proverbial bowl of cherries. Simply ignore the pits and they'll go away. . . right?

Now, such a mind set is not an illusion. It is sadly very real and is fully established by the time a child is 9 or 10. The power of advertising confirms this over and over. The whole idea revolves around the concept of "being" rather than"doing". The goal is to recognize being as a higher goal in and of itself - not as an abstract concept but rather as a lifestyle choice. The "doing" concept, on the other hand, is considered "old hat" - an annoying by-product of "tradition" - of a protestant work ethic. Doing is what we are stuck with until it's time for "thank god it's Friday".

## BEYOND DISCOURAGEMENT – CREATIVITY

Doing is passé, part of yesterday's belief system. Doing implies "work" and work is not "cool". "Being something" on the other hand, has become radically OK. Simply saying I want to be something now makes it so. It demands nothing from us. For example, I can, without skills or fear of reprisal, call myself a designer and even in some milieus a therapist - (forget that there are true versions of these professionals who do merit our respect). Just saying that I am what I want to be seems easy enough because in our society some "professions" are not considered "really that important". And even if some professions are considered somewhat important they aren't yet important enough to be regulated. In essence, some activities are basically "whatever" professions - i.e. expendable - things people can be without having to prove they really are. Unlike other professions which are peer and professional association controlled, mastering a skill related to these absconded with titles is not a requirement. As a prime example of this, many contemporary training programs in the visual arts no longer require drawing, painting or sculpting mastery in order to earn a Bachelor or Masters degree in Fine Arts. Forget neurologist Daniel Levitin's affirmation that:

> "... *in study after study, of composers, basketball players, fiction writers, ice-skaters, concert pianists, chess players ... it takes 10,000 hours before mastery can occur.*"

Never mind that this comment speaks of craft rather than art. Its premise is based on achieving excellence in a specific field. It reminds us that skill acquisition leads to assimilation of technique which then leads us to one day (possibly) "achieving" mastery in a specific domain - which *then* opens the door to a creative expression which can only be called: "Art". But mastering demands effort, concentration, practice, hard work ... possibly time spent as an apprentice and additional years of honing and mastering even further skills. But then, why bother when you can abscond with the status of "artist" without the hard work? No one would be the wiser... And no one really cares anyway.

Naturally, none of us would ever claim to be concert pianists, potters, podiatrists, engineers, architects or nuclear physicists. These professions demand not only the acquisition of skills but also their assimilation. And none of these activities could ever be associated with "easy".

Titles, which are free for the asking, generally come from those areas where the mysterious concept of "talent" reigns. Talent, it seems, is something certain special people have since birth. They have nothing to do with having it. They are just "lucky". And when you're "lucky" having this purported talent means you can crown yourself with that most revered of old titles: artist. Whether you merit this appellation or not isn't even questioned anymore. Why? Because few people actually know what is required to "do" artwork of a worthy nature. No one can say that you are not an artist if they don't know the difference between artworks that any dabbler can produce and "art" which is the realm of those rare persons who create that which achieves impact far and away beyond the ordinary.

Again, could you or I suddenly announce that we are now neuro-surgeons, linebackers with the Miami Dolphins, our boss's boss or dentists! We'd be laughed right out of the room if we bragged about such things. These are respected positions - recognized as being "impossible to achieve" without skill playing a major part in the expression of "our" innate talent.

Silliness aside. today's "valuable" mean-nothing titles are those which indiscriminately fulfill fantasies based on a long ago reverence for a position which was *once* not only held in awe but was deemed attainable only by a very special few. And that was so because excellence was once proof of a statement and status.

## When Nothing Is Something

In an environment where there is little respect for and at times no considered need for the learning and honing of skills, production values gradually falter. The longer excellence is denied, the sooner production takes on lowest common denominator characteristics which, at their lowest ebb, simply mimic "nothing". And nothing, at its Machiavellian best, is a pro at surreptitiously masking itself as "something". And when this occurs, "nothing" easily grows into an identity which, though it has no meaning, purpose or responsibility - does create a "status" for itself. When excellence of expression is no longer a requirement the validity of an easily absconded with title never has to fear being questioned.

When working well, doing our best, mastering or even trying are no longer prerequisites to successful functioning, a state of "permanent adolescence" or entitled irresponsibility establishes itself without opposition. Now, when I say permanent adolescence I don't wish to insult teenagers. More often than not the permanent adolescents in our midst are not those between 13 and 19. They are rather those who, in their 20s and 30s and 40s, work hard at only one thing: staying young and profiting from as much as they can for as long as they can. And from that contemporary ground swell, the concept of not growing up expands to include such behaviours as "children" in their 30s and 40s "going back home" - not to aid their aging parents but to once again depend on them in order to maintain specific lifestyles and avoid responsibility.

When responsibility and "growing up" are no longer core values or universally accepted norms, encouragement has a most difficult time helping to rebuild (i.e. to re-create) individual and communal emotional and mental infrastructures.

# Really?

When an environment promotes and celebrates how important it is "to be something" rather than to achieve something - nothing activities must eventually gain a status of "event". And the promotion of such events, more often than not, enters and pollutes our home environments through traditional means such as television ads and general as well as reality tv programming. Examples of the promoted concept of "nothing" in contemporary television are evident in such shows as Friends and Seinfeld. In the specific case of Seinfeld, the show promotes itself as being "about nothing", a display of nihilism where life is presented as pointless and where the characters are indifferent to the world outside their immediate circle. In the end, just "being friends" is sold as the ultimate state - i.e. a connection with communication rather than a communication with connection. In essence, commitment is feared if not totally denied. The contemporary nothing celebrated, therefore, becomes something through its rejection of emotional, mental or physical effort. What we once recognized as an unhealthy person's acceptance of a non-threatening existence over a daring (choosing) to live is now perceived as "normal". To "be" is to be. There is nothing else.

Doing something about the friendships portrayed in these sitcoms would actually "ruin the "nothingness of it all". Throughout the series, no happy endings take place. Things just go on ad infinitum. There is no beginning, middle or end to anything. Things just droningly "go on". In the end, Seinfeld was probably the first reality show. Its comedy had us laughing at the characters rather than being entertained by them.

Television advertising also plays by this contemporary rule of thumb, that is the concept of "being". In one particular advertisement, the presentation is rather subtle and difficult to criticize. It sells its product through a coyly presented public service announcement. It promotes the idea of "self-esteem in children" as a precious value. How can anyone criticize that? Nonetheless, it sends a message to children (little girls especially) that all they need do is "be" - proclaim themselves "beautiful" (before an adoring crowd of fantasy well-wishers) and accept that, by doing so, all is and will be well with the world.

Through this ad, the idea of existence - of simply "being" - (I am, therefore I am) is touted as wondrous and fulfilling and therefore gratifying - and therefore brings on happiness. And by surrounding this "nothingness" with an aura it suddenly becomes a marketable something. Simply considering oneself beautiful is "sold" as the basis for self-esteem - and this, it seems, is more important than working towards self-respect through the promotion of the acquisition of excellence. But where in the ad is this implied, you might ask? In the omission of the recognition of doing something to achieve something.

Whether we like it or not, accept it or not, the concept of "easy" and its concomitant "being" have been infiltrating our everyday lives for quite some time. And the symbiosis between virtual and real is at times quite shocking. As effort and struggling are increasingly relegated to a position of "antiquated thinking", there is a need to elevate every accomplishment, even trifle nothings, to a level of monumental event. For example: a tv ad's premise of being able "to go potty" is given (through musical crescendos and visual expressions of freedom) a comparable status to (let's say) graduating from high school. Translated into everyday life, children in many areas now wear caps and gowns upon leaving kindergarten and $1^{st}$ grade in order to celebrate "achievement"...

Now, toddlers are neither impressed nor disturbed by such get-ups and pseudo graduations (unless the tassels get in the way of plasticine wars). But these choreographed events seem to impact more on the "self-esteem" requirements of the significant adults in their lives than they do on the children's. But why? Reaching puberty as an important "event" far exceeds a 2 year old's pleasure at achieving a clean bottom or a 5 year old's "play graduation". But do we ever celebrate puberty as an important event? I should say not! Not only is that idea considered "primitive", the context and content of such a consideration has yet to be perceived by adults as a worthy subject to be discussed let alone celebrated. How ironic. Our world is so topsy-turvy, its logic can only be questioned.

Though we consider sex and violence in afternoon soap operas, early evening television news and programming as par for the course, we at the same time criticize the internet in our child's bedrooms as pernicious. For what? Introducing to them in a pornographic manner that which we refuse to present them in a loving and respectful manner?

And so, while our children go through a "real" event in their lives, we cringe at the very concept of celebrating that which will most effect the rest of their lives. . . The growing away from childhood and the entering into adolescence is a magical, mystical and even frightening phase in the life of children. They would really prefer not having to do it alone and even less having to go through the process based on the comments and actions of their peers who know no more and often less than they - who wish they knew more. Our celebrations of the banal (treating every silliness as fantastic, every nullity as worthy of note) emphasizes the great loss being experienced by our self-esteem era children who, as adults, will have little self-worth to base their lives on.

## Sameness Eroding Democracy

Having reached a time when what is valuable is no more important than what isn't, means that what we do or don't do takes on less and less moral implication or social responsibility. . . Nothingness, in all of its pseudo-pomp glory, becomes the only thing worthy of attention. It hides what is truly important. It veils truth in order to maintain a hold on a collectivity's soul.

In essence what we have accomplished through the minimization of achievement, through the concepts of "easy" and "being", is the dumbing-down of values and the elimination of individual thought under the guise of a more *democratic* universality of "being".

By rendering existence and self expression homogenous, we gradually eliminate individual creative effort. By selling the concept of "easy" to the masses we gradually kill whatever it is that makes us unique and powerful. But what we forget most is that this very destruction eliminates any ability we might have in the future to actually maintain this "easy" life we have created for ourselves. In essence, by destroying our capacity to create and to achieve and by celebrating egos rather than effort we are rendering ourselves vulnerable to eventual assimilation and subjugation.

Another serious consideration is that by focussing on "easy" we make achievement of any kind (or the lack of it) "personal". What does this mean?

What it means is that once everything worthy of consideration is deemed easy we are telling our children that there is no more room for failure. . . since why would anyone fail when everything presented to them has been deemed "easy". In and of itself, this is an anxiety laden prospect for any adult, let alone a child. And since children are not as naïve, they know that there is always a chance of failing at something or other. . . And then how do you explain yourself? How do you explain "failing" when everything is supposed to be simple? Failing in such a machinated environment is nothing more than a source of discouragement - a sign that we are less than others who don't fail.

Failing in such a scenario, makes an individual feel foolish rather than energized to seek solutions to a problem or question. Failing in an environment which promotes easy and being is so equated with being a loser, that it eventually is no longer associated in our minds with trying anew. And this means that a person has failed, rather than the action of trying.

When achievement, or the lack of it, is personal children soon realize that their self worth is threatened. Succeeding at all cost, all the time (though impossible for anybody to achieve) becomes crucial. Whether a specific challenge or other is worthy of their time and attention isn't important anymore. . . Failure "at anything" becomes the over-riding factor - and is at the same time no longer an option.

With this concept in place, a new element in child anxiety takes centre stage: being perceived as good (i.e. pleasing to others) over-rides doing well (i.e. being curious, daring, striving, achieving). When a child fears failing it is because any activity or action on their part is equated with "being" - with being who they are - with being bad or good - with being "I am a failure".

# BEYOND DISCOURAGEMENT – CREATIVITY

Enough… No More… - Graphite - 1984

*By the age of ten or eleven, many children have lost their innate curiosity to question, to scrutinize, to experiment, to discover. When a child fears failure, fears not being good enough, he or she falls into a sad adult-like silence of resignation which, even at that age, is excruciatingly palpable - 96*

And herein lies the link with easy. Many schools have introduced, no failure, no child left behind policies. Because of these concepts of over-simplification (in order to avoid hurting or traumatizing our perceived as delicate children) the creation of "homogeneity of success" is introduced. Children no longer need to "achieve" or "accomplish". They just have to "be" there, to be recognized. And if they do not achieve they are still recognized as being "successful" since the whole idea has more to do with salving adult consciences than it does with providing an honest environment in which learning and surviving can take place.

But children, in their most righteous selves, know full well that this is unadulterated blarney. Success, in such a context, is built on a framework of lies and cheating and fraud. And, it's not right to lie or cheat. . . is it?

But, with "easy succeeding" as the new and improved mantra and priority in our social and learning philosophies, we do what is required to "make it all happen". Living as victims of our environment rather than being daring individuals, we do not so much avoid the reality of trauma, pain, suffering or danger as we fear the "possibility" of them occurring. We alter achievement standards - eventually rendering them lowest common denominator - in order to allow children to "pass" - i.e. to avoid having to face "the possibility" of failing. And we do this to our children despite the obvious fact that in doing so we are preventing them from gaining the necessary tools to "really" move on.

And so with the personalization of everyday life activities become normal, such an attitude transforms the very word, meaning and practice of encouragement. Today, children are told how wonderful, beautiful and extraordinary they are when they accomplish little or absolutely nothing. For this is the new "something". We no longer speak of accomplishment. We only speak of the child "being a child" as paramount. The fact that they "are" is an achievement in and of itself. We hand out awards and certificates and trophies like candy. . . not for doing but for being - for being who they are, for being "there", for being cute, for smiling, sitting, standing, going potty - i.e. for being willing to "be" whatever it is we need them to be.

God forbid that our children would have to strive and squirm in their seats and try and try and try again before achieving victory. That would mean that they would become strong - able to deal

## BEYOND DISCOURAGEMENT – CREATIVITY

with things on their own. And today, we prefer our children vulnerable, innocent and, well: children. We perceive them as being in need of a never-ending special guidance - a hovering supervision and a protection based on "what ifs" rather than real life. This we do, not because we are afraid of the fateful day when they will leave us but rather we are afraid for ourselves. We fear making mistakes, erring in judgement, having our children hurt their shins, their knees, their noses, their feelings because we will be perceived as " not being up for the game". In essence we are afraid of "failing" at parenthood and having the finger pointed at us. Such is the realm of personalized existence.

And how can we not feel embarrassed when our children don't measure up, fall and hurt themselves. How can we not feel like failures when our children don't make it in school or constantly act out? After all of the guidance we constantly receive from the powers that be, the specialists, the social workers, the psychologists, the pharmaceutical experts? Why are WE still failing? It's all supposed to be easy, isn't it?

Sadly, our role as parents, teachers and mentors has become one of helping children avoid any and all pain, any and all pratfalls, any and all bumps in the road - even those which are necessary to assure they can successfully survive in a tough world.

> *When the Creator asked us to be childlike, not once did that ever mean we should be dependent, innocent, naive, or submissive. God created children and adults to be vibrant, curious, giving, taking, daring, caring, . . . Most of all, we have all been put on this earth to be creative. - 83*

But as stated previously, children are not naïve... They know that all of this "let's make everything easy", "lets homogenize parenting and childhood and school and sports." - all of it... is just so much horse padoody. They may not see it intellectually as dangerous but their feelings are real. Children sense "real" danger. And they are frightened. A child knows instinctively that notions of "facile" are dangerous - not to some sham form of commercialized self esteem - but to their overall sense of fulfilment and self-worth. In essence, children don't really know what is going on but they do "feel" deep down inside that they are being prevented from growing and becoming the powerful entities they were meant to be. But how can this be, if all of this is about assuring them a healthy "self-esteem"?

*Being a good parent does not mean telling our children to "be" something - it is encouraging them to "do" something... and to cheer them on when difficulties arise. - 07*

## Verbal Revisionism

Once, self-esteem defined how we felt about ourselves as "functional" beings. Therefore its "old" definition related more to the value we gave ourselves as it related to our position in the rest of the world. Today, it speaks to our need for recognition - much as a newborn demands recognition from another as "special" - above all else. Today's self esteem speaks more to an encounter of the self in the mirror than it does about the value of the self per se. In essence, self-esteem has been manipulated, altered, redefined to suit a more contemporary "me-ness". And along with this new life-concept, the very idea of encouragement has been manipulated and trivialized.

# BEYOND DISCOURAGEMENT – CREATIVITY

Encouragement once meant that we, as adults, provided an environment in which children could launch themselves into the unknown without fear that their safety net would disappear. A child could live life without being afraid of trying new and exciting things. But as previously noted, the very word and concept of encouragement (amongst others) has suffered seriously from the ill-effects of our era's penchant for opportunistic revisionism.

Not so long ago, words had finite definitions. Specific words meant specific things. We didn't have to think about word meanings. They meant what they meant. Hence, someone's word was their bond. Today, definitions and ideas are in a constant state of flux where anything can mean anything as long as we all succumb to the "new and improved" (and more often than not) commercial redefinition...

Very little consideration, time or effort are being spent to analyse how we articulate this new environment we've created for ourselves - and more especially for our children. But in the end, we all pay. The very words we use today say much about us. When a lax mental and emotional perspective on the part of a society grafts onto words a power they should not have, the whole of a community is affected. When words suddenly redefine perspectives, to suit a declining effort in the area of individual and community values, the consequences can be dire. In essence, how we use words moulds the way we all come to think, feel, share and participate... or not, in what life has to offer.

That many words adapt to meet the needs of a new era is nothing new to language. I am not criticising the changes which naturally occur over time. Language is always in a state of "becoming". My concern has more to do with words which do not so much evolve as they are manipulated by short term self-interest groups and fads whose logic or goals care little for long term effects or human standards.

Today, words are revised to suit the needs of a consumer and objectification based environment. In essence, the medium is no longer the message - illusion is.

> *It is a lie that we are more communicative, better informed than in the past. A heavier dose of lowest common denominator stimulation does not constitute a more informed mind, a more substantive thought, a more caring viewpoint. It simply makes it more palatable. . . more politically correct, more "user friendly". - 99*

## What I Said Was. . . Wasn't It?

The following table describes the extent to which premature and arbitrary redefinition and revisionism play havoc with perceptions. Words which once meant one thing seem to have been altered to mean an equal and opposite definition - or at worst, to have gained a meaning they were never meant to have. The lowest common denominator revisions not only highlight our contemporary "word-dystrophy" but also indicate strongly how individual and community perceptions can be moulded. This list does not so much indicate that the English language is threatened. Rather, it shows how "easy" it is to disturb emotional and mental well being through the manipulation of common communication tools in an environment.

## BEYOND DISCOURAGEMENT – CREATIVITY

*Today... we read*
*change as progress*
*charm as authenticity*
*common sense as naïveté*
*compensation as satisfaction*
*demands as rights*
*existing as living*
*growth as progress*
*homogenization as globalization*
*insult as honesty*
*infatuation as love*
*invasion as liberation*
*kitsch as creative*
*obsession as passion*
*overprotection as love*
*licence as freedom*
*perfection as excellence*
*nude as naked*
*revisionism as history*
*discipline as abuse*
*narcissism as ego*
*criticism as critiquing*
*tolerance as respect*
*opinion as fact*
*victim as hero*

If we but analyse one word from this list - let's say the word "victim", it is easier to comprehend the nature of verbal revisionism and the dangers inherent in its practice. Being a "victim" was once associated with having suffered an unexpected and/or uncontrollable attack or harm at the hands of another person, place or event. To be a victim was to "temporarily" find oneself in a more than difficult situation. A victim was someone who was in need of support, empathy AND encouragement in order to overcome the effects of a suffering not of their own making.

In essence, victimhood was a devastating time through which a human being was forced to pass - not a state of being into which a person felt compelled to stay. Today, we seem to perceive victimhood as a quasi-permanent state of affairs. We are even prodded by certain helping professions to perceive it as a state which, for all intents and purposes, is impossible (or nearly so) to overcome - (at least without ongoing, long-term, specialized help). . . Essentially, victimhood has become a sanctioned and even promoted state of being where an individual becomes the dependent of an environment which seems to benefit from that dependency.

It is through the revisionism (arbitrary imposition of definitions and attitudes) that victimhood becomes "sealed" as a "profitable" state of being for some and a quasi-permanent prison sentence for others. And as such, it is often awarded the reverential descriptive of "heroic". Why? Where once heroism defined a person who overcame adversity, it now defines a person who "submits" to an in perpetuity state of environment-sanctioned martyrdom.

And as is the case in most mutilations of perspective, it is always *true* victims (i.e. the real - and not made up) who suffer most from having their real pain trivialized by the new and improved lowest common denominator definition victimhood now espouses.

BEYOND DISCOURAGEMENT – CREATIVITY

## Come On Down!

With victimhood gone mainstream its value, both as a commercially promotable product and as a target audience, increases. Contemporary entertainment has shown itself to not be shy in the use of anything and everything which has the capacity to entice or to lure new audiences. Partnered with focussed advertising, such programming deals itself a winning hand. As previously stated, victimhood gone mainstream gives discouraged individuals a false sense of belonging, of recognition, of acceptance and even of stardom. Add to this the excessive television promotion and sale of stimulants and depressants to deal with every "victimhood perceived" ache and pain - and we have another key element in this era's sanctioning of discouragement.

Revisionism in verbal communication is therefore not of little consequence. How we use words or perceive their meanings does play a role in defining how we act, react, encourage and. . . discourage. The implementation and daily use of redefined words lead to misconceptions, perplexed mind sets and the "whatever" attitudes our children and adolescents throw back at us.

But overall, the misuse and abuse of words and their meanings are not the total picture. They represent but one sign that our living environment is not as healthy as it should be.

## Laugh
## And The World Laughs With You

With words no longer meaning what they say and "easy" being the new byword it becomes "normal" to seek out what is effortless - not only during those times when we are expected to "work" but also during our leisure hours. A case in point is the invention of and soon become universal acceptance of television as an entertainment medium. From the very beginning, the idea of controlling the time and interests of not only small communities but whole countries was a heady experience for producers of television programs. The public en masse would drop everything they were doing to pass the time sitting before this virtual new world of pleasurable experience. But was this consideration of mass concentration a reality or an illusion? How could this theory of actual "mass submission" (which could certainly lead to larger and larger profits) be proven?

The single most powerful tool came about in 1950 when the "laugh-track" was introduced to television sitcoms. Through this invention, television programmers could dictate to the world at large not only what was funny but when they should laugh, how long they should laugh and how hard they should laugh. Before the laugh track, an audience was king. It decided whether a program was successful or not, whether a family would sit before a television screen or not. Bad comedy wasn't good for business. So, laugh tracks actually came about to homogenize laughter - to control the freedom individuals have to decide what is or is not funny, what is or is not good entertainment.

With canned laughter, audiences no longer waited to mentally analyse a punch line for its quality anymore. They, like Pavlovian subjects, began to wait for the first split-second sound of a laugh track to "tell" them if, when and how much amusement they should express. From the moment this control discovery was made, mass entertainment took on a life of its own. And no audience since has ever been perceived as a group of intelligent consumers. With the acceptance of laugh-tracks as natural as sunrise, viewers became pliable and manipulatible subjects. The rest is history.

In the beginning of this new century, nothing much has changed. Though computer monitors are gradually increasing their audience base in the entertainment arena, television still reigns supreme as the main source of mass attraction. Actually, television is in a reincarnation phase. Even before its purported demise, it re-invented its news and entertainment formats along with its "bigger is better" monitor configurations. And, as younger audiences are prone to segregating themselves from the mainstream, the powers that be are once again in the forefront of adaptation. With the increasing numbers of individual communication devices showing no signs of abating, programming is quickly adapting itself to meet this new demographic's demands. And what are the demands of this new generation of "viewers"?

## Side-Show Freaks

By far the greatest attraction, in this first part of the 21$^{st}$ century, is the side-show antics of reality television programming. The premises are universal no matter the broadcaster - i.e. comedy, tragi-comedy or soap opera-style shows are all eerily similar in their presentations. They all focus on or highlight weakness or the idiocy of as many human frailties as possible.

Victimhood, self-imposed or not, is in. Failings are sold to us as more interesting and "attractive" than talents or accomplishments and more titillating than nightly sitcoms. The whole television environment has locked on to programming which is production-cheap and income high . As luck would have it. . . . this new and improved entertainment is reminiscent of past carnival and local fair freak-shows - where physical deformities were the lowest common denominator attractions of the day. Cruelly offered up as gawking entertainment is in. The attraction is the same as yesteryear: for a few pennies we could point a finger at the displayed "freaks".

Today, the same gratuitous promoter attitudes prevail. Viewers become willing voyeurs. The ads take our money and we get the privilege of being titillated by the frayed edges of souls whose failed lifestyles, mental and emotional deformities and wayward personalities outweigh our own as yet undisclosed disabilities. And as we sit, beer and popcorn in hand, we both smile and wince, convincing ourselves how much better we are than these televised "freaks".

To get our attention, reality television started with a bang. So-called star-level hosts were called upon to highlight what can only be labelled "disturbing if not disturbed" behaviours. Once hooked, audiences become feeding frenzy regulars. Eventually though, the shows gradually toned themselves down - without abandoning their new found cash cow.

Re-calibrated, reality shows now "appear" less chaotic, in the bizarre sense, and more and more "real" in a revisionist sense. And this is where "reality television" begins in earnest. Races and challenges, falsely described as "true to life" adventures and experiences, highlight "likable" losers. Winners seemingly appear as incidental props to the "real" show - which is discovering who the next "loser" will be. Who will "fail in the race - be rejected, be "gotten rid of".

At this point, audiences are well trained in the "appreciation" of the odd, the weird and the sickly. And with the acceptance of victimhood as "normal" entertainment, we find ourselves watching more and more sophisticated reality shows. . . Rarely are "bizarre" people highlighted anymore. Now, "normal" families are paraded - displaying their private emotions, disabilities, psychological and marital failings, dysfunctional children - for all the world to see. We're not watching basic eccentrics play out their antics. We are now vicariously inside "real" people's homes. . . purportedly to "encourage" their healing, to sympathize and empathize with their multiple pains, to offer "intervention' and, since nothing is free, to voyeuristically be titillated by their exhibitionistic sufferings.

Delving into the dirty linen of virtual "neighbours" is the new entertainment. And though we now supposedly know what goes on behind closed doors, we still fail in one respect. Being amateur voyeurs, we fail to recognize that "1984" is not the monstrous, elusive Big Brother we think him to be.

*He is us...*

And so, by highlighting "heroic losers" - considering them worthy of attention and praise, we have learned to integrate ridicule, sneering and belittling into our socially acceptable lexicon of norms. And sitting at our feet, watching this same entertainment and taking in our every sneer, our every derision are our children. And below their mimicked adult-like bravado - if you look carefully - you see fear in their eyes. . . fear that one day, someone will see them as worthy of being sneered at and belittled - just for the fun of it. And how, pray tell, after all of this discouragement is pummelled into their minds, are we to teach them about warmth and generosity, giving and sharing, excellence and creativity?

## The Fear Factor

Through the above-mentioned venues, presented at all hours in family environments, children learn that ridiculing, criticism and sneering are tantamount to objective critiquing. The focus on who is to be the next "loser" eventually overpowers the higher human instincts required to offer good wishes to contestants or to even consider the proverbial: "May the best contestant win!". After awhile we no longer vote for a winner but are rather turned on by the process of elimination in which those who just might be the next to lose find themselves.

In a discouraged environment "pointing the finger at" and at the same time celebrating a loser (from the virtual realms of television and computerland) give us the false impression that we are actually playing a "controlling" part in determining what is success and what is failure, what is good and what is bad, what is real and what is not. What we fail to realize is that after awhile we function under the illusion that our home environments are safe havens - separate from those television personalities we have so easily determined to be "less than we are". In essence, the foundation for this illusion is built on the premise that no one "out there" will ever look our way when the search is on to find the next "wondrous' loser.

In the past few generations we have gradually built up an environment of subtle identification with discouragement through sanctioned derision. Celebrating the best we can be is no longer a marketable product. Pain sells longer. Winning doesn't do. Losing sells more. We would rather now"laugh at" than laugh with or look up to another.

And the various derisive comments we found ourselves making so easily about those weird television "others" we now find are easy to make about those closest to us. . . teasingly of course. . . And when we are surprised that feelings are hurt. . . The only retort seems to be: "Well, come on, now. . . Lighten up! "I'm just having some fun!" or the now most acceptable inanity: "I'm just trying to be honest!"

But, as Richard Needham points out:

*Those who say they are simply being brutally honest are more interested in brutality than in honesty.*

# BEYOND DISCOURAGEMENT – CREATIVITY

In the end, we live in an era where "pointing out the bad teeth of a person - rather than noticing their friendly smile"- is considered a healthy response to another. And for children this is both "very" educational and extremely frightening. For they can only desperately hope and pray that everyone continues to point a finger at others - point to another's frailties, errors, silliness, faults, mistakes, failures . . . not theirs.

Though reality tv cannot be blamed for the whole picture, its voyeuristic brutal honesty at best and its comedic-pornography at worst certainly play an important role in establishing for our children what is and is not acceptable behaviour. They are affected by this "normal" in our choices of entertainment. And when our choices include being titillated by demeaning behaviour, dysfunctionality and emotional brutality it should not be surprising that our children are suffering more and more from anxiety and fear of others. Are these fears exaggerated? I doubt it. What is the number one problem in our schools today? What is the major complaint of parents and students? Lack of facilities? Lack of funding? Lack of good teachers? No. The main problem as far as children are concerned is bullying. And that leaves us with only one question: At school and on the playground, which role will be our child's? That of the bully or that of the victim?

What we and our children get from life is often all we have to offer back. Is a philosophy of discouragement being used to raise our children? Is the best that we offer them nothing more than titillation or avoidance of dread? Or is all that I have put forth simply an exaggeration or undue worry about life simply being itself. . . a "modern" society with new "values" and "mores"?

BERNARD POULIN

# Lowered Expectations, Lost Horizons

Though smaller than we are, and younger, children are the inevitable harbingers of how healthy our societal systems are. And life, it seems, is definitely wrapping us up in worries. We worry about money, life, health, age, bills, insurance, relationships, children, partners, wars, what others think, how others perceive us, how fat, how thin, how beautiful or ugly we are. We worry about dirt and hidden germs, terror and anxieties of aging and still not knowing "who we are" - fearing every stranger who smiles at us - or worse - at our children. Every tree seems to hide a monster, every corner a thief, every day another worry. But as we want better for our children, we strive to protect them from every bug, person and tragedy life might offer. We hate what we're stuck doing for a living and fear that our children will also - and so, we protect them from having to deal with anything that smacks of work or difficulty or stress. We can't abide that they are tested, questioned or challenged.

From birth, we fill their rooms, our rooms, all rooms in the house with massive amounts of toys and games. We fill their hours with an excessive amount of organized activities, play-dates and learning experiences. We leave little if any time for them to simply be children. And being children is almost a lost art due to every second of their lives being assaulted by an army schedule of child-centered, gender-neutral, self-esteem based concepts which do little more for children than drive them literally around the bend. And so, little if any time is left in our lives - or theirs - to simply and without artifice communicate and share and enjoy each other.

# BEYOND DISCOURAGEMENT – CREATIVITY

And as this is more and more prominent in the lexicon of contemporary life, why are we at all perplexed by children and adolescents displaying entitlement, lack of self-discipline and self-confidence, anxiety, fear, anger, frustration and brutality issues? Why do we get upset when children act out or are excessively dependent, irresponsible, have poor communication skills or are unable to make decisions? Why is it normal today for parents to be upset with teachers when their child misbehaves at school? Why has it become acceptable when children are belligerent, disrespectful, irreproachable, demanding, selfish and disconnected from those closest to us?

When children are at the point of holding sway over how and what they will do, not do, want or not want, learn or not learn the future bodes poorly for us all. Outgrowing "immature" behaviour does not just go away on its own. Considering oneself superior and entitled does not end with childhood.

Leslie Manion, an Ottawa College professor, quite simply reflects the point of this book and the feelings of many college and university professors when she points out:

> *"If elementary and high school students have not acquired throughout their years at school the right combination of knowledge and discipline they are automatically ill prepared for college or university and subsequently the future labour force.*
>
> *After having 12 years of spoon-feeding, self-esteem building and lackadaisical attitudes that include no failure, no penalties, and no deadline policies, many students are rudely awakened when they get into a college setting. Punctuality and regular attendance, both highly valued commodities in the workplace, appear to be options by the time students enter higher education. Expectations of special treatment abound. And, because they think quite highly of their own*

*skills and abilities and have rarely been criticized, challenged or tested, they are shocked when they get Cs and Ds or worse, fail. Today's high school students definitely are better informed than ever before. However, they come out of the high school system immature, dependent, with an attitude of entitlement and lacking basic skills. Society as a whole is one day going to suffer greatly for this."*

Generic parental and societal demands of the day, fed by an insatiable pocket psychology book market, dictates that children should be protected from most if not all demands on their person. Over the past century this has caused a major rift between parents and children as well as home and school environments. Children, when discouraged define their responsibilities as nil, their privileges as rights and their control of the home and school environments as quasi total.

They are looking for order and security. And finding none, they simply take over where the reigns have fallen.

Upset, at this state of affairs, we adults try to turn the tables by focussing more and more intently on calming the children and blaming ourselves for being inadequate. In essence the whole situation increasingly resembles the analogy of the blind leading the blind or the more mundane: walking around evermore in circles.

Schools, to meet the new demands of child-centered obsessions, have been ordered to manipulate or tone down expectations. The results are environments of pseudo- comfort (if not boredom) which lead to children failing but passing nonetheless and knowing less than is required for them to move on with pride and self-assurance. And so. . . under such a soft mandate, children assume that no one is actually steering the ship. And, when angry outbursts fail to make the required changes in adult attitudes, they eventually turn off and tune out. They retreat. They become lost, distraught and depressed. It is at this stage that children abandon themselves to the waiting arms of the less frustrating virtual world of their digital gadgetry.

In reality, what we create through all of this chaos are very angry children who feel the need to exercise power where no leadership exists. As stated in the first pages of this chapter, life and creativity cannot exist in a vacuum. A fertile ground needs to be in place if living beings are to flourish. Children sense this. When little of what they need is readily available to them, they quickly get the impression that the significant adults in their lives have abandoned their responsibilities as parents and teachers. When their environment lacks the courage to be strong for them, children feel unsafe and incapable of being the best they can be. So why stay "connected"?

## Basic Instincts

By the age of 5, 7 or 11, disconnected-from-reality children begin to find that direct sharing and communication is uncomfortable. To these astronauts-of-virtual-space, direct communication is an annoyance at best, a threat to their running-away-from-it-all at worst. Being "connected" to a digital soother gradually becomes their "real" and only safe world when times are fuelled by anxiety.

In 1989, Berlin tore down its wall of separation and disconnection. Twenty years later the children of the west are building walls of protective isolation from a world filled with and run on license they can no longer abide.

## Beam Me Up Scotty

Abhorring direct one on one communication is becoming a fact, a norm. Is it any wonder that when a real live person "interrupts" a technologically self-exiled child that this individual reacts angrily, even aggressively? It is no surprise that children, when spoken to - during times they deem "theirs" - feel imposed upon - their private space invaded. Trying to suddenly reach an eleven year old - to ask them to integrate, when his or her whole life has been one of little if any connection, is a rather discouraging task.

Not long ago, I was invited to speak to a grade 7 class about my life as a painter. I asked the teacher if the children were allowed electronic equipment during class hours. She replied that it certainly was not policy to allow students to plug into their personal music and texting paraphernalia - but that it was "difficult to stop them". . . especially when faced with a stranger - a new face offering information with which they are unfamiliar. . . She definitely was uncomfortable with the look on my face, as I took in this incredibly ridiculous information. I politely declined the invitation to visit this class where children have usurped and retain the power to "disengage" if they choose to - where children are no longer curious or interested. To think that I could have changed such mind sets during a one hour session would have been ludicrous. 12 and 13 students. . . and they are already controlling the environment from which they are purportedly being offered the skills to not only survive but thrive as adults? Amazing!!! When children give themselves permission to "push away reality" whenever they please, what does this say about our system structures - be they academic or familial? What does it say about our children's capacity to be fully alive and creative and pleasured by life's offerings?

Children want to please and be pleased. But. . . not in an environment which doesn't know what it wants for and from itself or for and from them. And since this situation is often overwhelming for children, their "run-away" solution may be "child-like" but it sure beats our "childish" adult responses to the messes we find ourselves in. Children often retreat into worlds which allow them time to rebuild their strengths. But when no satisfaction or responsible adult is at hand to handle what is already not a child's responsibility, they eventually just stay in retreat.

The digital wonders of the day are often "outs" from the perplexing situations in which today's children constantly find themselves. And so, expert finders-of-solutions that children are, they use technology not as a tool but rather as a cosy dark closet where they can envelop themselves in an illusion of comfort.

When children feel that what is out there is no longer interested in meeting their needs, nor allowing them recognition or growth - they first get upset. When that solves nothing, they hide. Children, at this stage of discouragement, give up on trying because there is no environment of security. It seemed to be there when they were little but no longer appears to have the strength nor the will to be there for them now. And the older children get in such a head and heart space, the more frightened, the more angry and the more depressed they become.

## Creativity Denied

When afraid, children often don't know why. They may not define clearly what is an affront to them but they sense it as being wrong and anxiety provoking. In the end, when such a burden is too heavy to cope with, even the saving grace of creativity begins to fail them.

With encouragement nothing more than a faded promise, creativity becomes less and less possible and eventually less and less important. And when that devastating scar appears on the souls of children, the strength to stand up for themselves fades. The day of reckoning, for we adults - the real sign that our children will have been damaged beyond repair - is the day they no longer fight us. When children would rather disappear completely into their world of self-protection - deflated and defeated, we have not only lost them, they have lost themselves. For, once ensconced in that nebulous world of "whatever", it is difficult to extricate children or give them back their right to a creative self.

## Stepping Up To The Plate

But then. . . Is it not elitist to offer our children more than is democratically acceptable - more than normal expectations of the day - even if those expectations are lowest common denominator? Is it not harmful to subject them to possible failure in their quest to reach ever greater heights? Are we selling them a dream, a fantasy that when un-attained, will cause upset to them?

Shouldn't having what everyone else has be enough? Actually, enough is never enough. Offering up the possibility of reaching ever greater heights is not a fantasy. It is a quest, a dream of going beyond the beyond. Children need to dream, to wish for, to strive and to reach out. Without these, they shrivel and shrink and become less than they are.

But keeping children safe and secure (i.e,. dependent) is nothing less than a call to arms today. We are constantly bombarded with a 24 hour a day media blitz which thrives on news reports of danger, accidents, bombings, wars, crimes, diseases and dark streets where "strangers" lurk. News is piped into our homes 24/7 and the more glitz added to the "facts" the better. News is no longer information, it is the entertainment sandwiched between reality shows.

# BEYOND DISCOURAGEMENT – CREATIVITY

Whether the daily depicted horrors are natural disasters or man-made wars is irrelevant. The images displayed often overshadow the descriptive dialogue. First we look and then look away frightened as, in turn, our children are. Eerily, because we are so marked by these never-ending programmed encounters with devastation, a new form of profiteering arises - one which plays on our overwhelmed feelings. Numerous faceless "non-profit"organizations suddenly spring from nowhere - playing on our anxieties with their never-ending calls for funds "to save our children, our animals, our world". Via newspapers, magazines, the internet, television infomercials and posted pamphlets, they never let up - reminding us of the ever-present dangers, horrors and debilitations that lurk. Eager volunteers and Hollywood stars are called upon to personalize the spread of "scary details" - so often based on nebulous reports and manipulated statistics. And the moneys roll in. . .

> *Loving parents guide their children through the minefields of life - all the while stifling the urge and their fears to completely smooth out the road before them. - 97*

How else are we to feel but frightened and worried? Real events are not just presented, they are "produced and directed" for maximum visual and emotional impact. Like dramatic sitcoms, every one of the world's pains is broadcast to us "live" - canned for viewing in between targeted ads. These, in turn, sell us products to calm our modern-day woes or to "help us" sleep like a baby or to simply avoid the tensions of everyday life which "just might" be handicapping us. . .

As parents, teachers and mentors maybe it's time we question those who would have us frightened all the time. Maybe we want the world our children live in to be less focussed on the promotion of what is bad and more on the encouragement of what is possible. But is there room for such basic traditional ideas?

## Updating Encouragement

Encouragement is a concept which needs to be examined in a new light. - a light emphasizing the qualities of life rather than the "symptoms" we have been told are reminiscent of our true natures. To be a supportive partner in the area of child creativity parents, teachers and mentors need to rediscover the natural rather than the therapeutic values which make up healthy humanity and relationships.

Admittedly, the very word "encouragement" lacks a microchip aura. In this world where every banal or insipid occasion is a happening and every gratification instant, it is difficult to conceive of old fashioned encouragement being a solution to anything.

But, with the $21^{st}$ century seemingly out to maintain the 20th's creation of institutionalized victimhood, something needs to be done to rid ourselves of this debilitating "voyeur cum masochistic" attitude of the century. The very idea of seeing ourselves as "normally suffering" - as in need of constant therapeutic or pharmaceutical intervention must be dealt with. Ending up as continents of addled and addicted dependents is not an option. But to regain our humanity - our imperfect yet healthy normality - the reintegration of encouragement in our daily lives is vital.

Children need to see life as a process, whereby the search for excellence and contentment is an adventure, not a punishment. They must not only know this as good but also as their right. If child-centeredness must revolve around something it should revolve around this. Children must know that life has pain but is not pain-filled. They need to know that life is not fair but nonetheless offers everyone possibilities.

Now, this is not to say that some of us, whether adults or children, do not normally have a difficult time of it - do not suffer from various debilitating difficulties. Some of us do. Some of us have ongoing mental, emotional or physical issues which demand therapeutic or medicinal assistance. There is no denying of that fact. But these are the few - the real victims in our society who seem to be ignored because we have made victimhood generic - popular even. And by doing this, we pooh-pooh those who truly are suffering from difficulties which make living well harder than for most.

Children need to know this and be aware that life challenges different people in different ways. Recognizing that creative life is possible "despite" pain and adversity is life-saving information for all children to have. It is in this very fact that a child comes to realize that NOTHING can stop creativity if the environment is encouraging.

The creative process must be seen as a proactive act of growth and spiritual sustenance. Creativity is a stimulant which allows individuals of any age to take on the world *despite* sufferings, desperation, sadness and hurts, NOT because of them. Creativity is a process of the brave, not the victim. We must stop seeing ourselves and our children as hurt or potentially hurt individuals who must over-protect and be over-protected.

Life is neither heaven nor hell nor is it even purgatory. Life is a miracle filled with wonders to be discovered, pleasures to be felt and pains to be overcome. Yes, it is true, life hurts at times. But creativity builds strengths - the strengths required to face and stand up to adversity. Creativity is a builder of power, an eliminator of weakness. And children need to be offered that type of encouragement - that type of strength.

In essence, I don't believe that most of the population of North America is sick. It is simply discouraged. Taking charge, deciding, choosing and moving ahead in order to offer our children the best that we can be (both for ourselves and for them) is a choice to be made, a choosing to act rather than a do nothing submission.

Naturally, we can't expect that all of the problems of the day will simply go away. They won't. But we can do our best to take back our parental, teaching and mentoring prerogatives. And one of these is dealing with everyday problems as just that - problems to be dealt with one-by-one and overcome one-by-one.

## Sometimes

Sometimes solving a problem is simple - but discouragement often pushes us into using the same useless problem solving techniques over and over - and nothing ever gets better. Sometimes, we just need encouragement to see life differently - to see it in a more positive light - and by doing so to become more creative in our problem solving techniques.

> *As a teenager, I worked as a "picker" and farmhand in the summer. I spent many an end of day cleaning "cow residue" from my boots. It would take some time to accomplish and the smell was rather intense. Every evening the farmer sat on the porch, watching me clean my boots. . . Finally, after a week of this, he simply said: "Cows walk by that same spot every day. . . You walk by there everyday. . . If you take the time to clean that area before you walk into it you might spend 5 minutes shovelling it into the manure pile rather than every day a ½ hour cleaning it off your boots."*

# BEYOND DISCOURAGEMENT – CREATIVITY

Sometimes we need to look less negatively at a situation and more positively at a potential solution. A case in point is that of the revered Van Gogh. In reading and musing about his life, how many of us have focussed primarily on pitying him, on highlighting his sufferings and his pain. How many of us have made a hero of him *because* "his suffering" caused him to create beautiful paintings? Sadly, we are the lesser for belittling his determination.

Van Gogh painted the world in a most extraordinary and unique way. He did this majestically not because he suffered, not because there was no interest in his work or because there were no sales to be had, but *despite* all of these problems. Van Gogh painted despite his pain not because of it. What we should be focussing on in regards to a man such as him is that he did so because he was not only self-encouraging but he was also encouraged by his loving brother Theo to be the best he could be - despite the drawbacks in his life.

To read the letters between the brothers is to discover a beautiful relationship of love and hope - of encouragement. Such power of creativity, overcoming great odds, is the type of heroism a child needs to know about - not the cult of victimhood which taints this desperate era of ours. Children should feel that this is also their due - to be encouraged to go on - despite anything which dares stand in their way.

But, as has been discussed from the beginning, discouragement, more than strangers, lurks in the dark corners of our environments. It is a poison which destroys courage and saps the energy of both children and adults. Its only goal is to overtake and eliminate the strength and creativity of every individual. Why is this? Possibly we live in a time and space of discouragement. Possibly the context in which we live is not conducive to good mental and emotional health or creativity. And so - just maybe - it's time to analyse it - to do something about it for our own sake and that of our children.

# 2
## The Context

Jour d'été - Graphite - 6" x 3"

*The constant craving to render easy everything we do is the very act by which we ultimately destroy all vestiges of human creative potential. - 01*

## The Environment

We live in an era of unstable teaching and child-rearing techniques. Consistency is an anomaly. We are obsessed with change and *newness* - forget that results are achieved or not. We cannot abide, or so it seems, that something which worked "yesterday" would ever fit into the era in which we now live. Old is bad and, oddly, old is not even "the distant past" but rather "just minutes ago". But what has all of this to do with how children look at and handle life? What has it to do with creativity?

Well, a specific time provides a context - an environment in which our children grow. And in this particular era, children as a group present as anxious, nervous, dependent, insecure and, in ever-increasing numbers, depressed - and all of these at an ever younger age. Physically, the situation is rather frightening. Our children are less and less healthy. They eat excessively and the wrong foods. And their lifestyle is too sedentary to promote good health in either the short or long term. The number of children who fall into the category of obesity is staggering. The problem is so serious that type 2 diabetes, high blood pressure, high cholesterol, back problems and childhood asthma are on the rise. Over the past three decades obesity rates have more than doubled for preschool children aged 2 to 5 and adolescents aged 12 to19 years. The rate has more than tripled for children 6 to11. In total, over 9 million 6 to 19 year old children in the United States are overweight or obese. Rates in Canada are similar: 26% of children (2-17) are currently overweight or obese. The pressure that this situation imposes on a society is dangerously close to rendering a large portion of that population dysfunctional. Now it would be dishonest to put all the blame in one basket. A sedentary lifestyle is not enough to render a child obese, though it is a major contributing factor.

# BEYOND DISCOURAGEMENT – CREATIVITY

Anxiety and other emotional problems are also players when it comes to pushing a child to cope with life in whatever fashion it takes to "calm the nerves". And when children eat to soothe themselves, discouragement is already defining how their lives unfold. It also affects children in many other ways - among them: lack of energy, excessive energy, loss of interest in learning and growing, lethargic responses to any stimulation. And when children no longer find life enjoyable, no longer are curious or excited or passionate about anything - they are in trouble. And they are that way because the load they are carrying is just too heavy.

What is often overlooked, where children are concerned, is their desire to lighten "our" load - their capacity to feel our pain - their need to try to eliminate it in their own loving ways. Over and above their own personal worries, children easily take on (as my wife says) the colour of their surroundings. Being sensual, children not only feel their own hurts they also sense the insecurity oozing from the pores of their parents and teachers. And this adds to feelings of being lost in a fog - of being unable to deal with the hand that is dealt. And so, children compensate in one form or another. Whether it is through eating, not eating, fading into the background, playing video games deep into the night until sleep eventually takes over. . . Anything is worth a try when pains of varied or unknown origins are just too much to handle.

> *Depression is to fall into a deep sleep and to no longer want to awaken - to do what once we did lovingly - 01*

When no solution is evident, i.e. when months of worry, aggression, rebellion or other forms of negative behaviour don't work - these "normal" reactions eventually subside. But this is not to say that all is well with the world. Rather than be celebrated, this calm before the storm is more a sign of apathy and retreat. And such a total discouragement is possible because, today, we have the technological gadgetry which allows us to pull back, turn off, ignore, participate no more - if this is what we want.

And yet, despite these increasing signs of ill health in our children we continue to submit them and ourselves to unproven, unwise and uncreative rearing techniques - techniques geared more to selling "ever newer ideas" and "just ask your doctor" behaviour modification drugs than to introducing any real solution. In essence we have come to trust the "untrustable" because we are at a point where we don't or won't even trust ourselves. Needless to say, behind a consumer-based façade of all is well, contemporary family dynamics are in a rut. Our "modern" times have created increasing numbers of anxious parents and more and more distraught teachers - to say nothing of children desperately hanging onto any secure hold they can manage.

But there is some hope, if common sense attitudes promoted by the world's "free-range kids" movements are any indication. Some parents, it seems, are getting it. . . They have had it with trying to be perfect. They want their lives back. They want better for their children. And they don't want to be dictated to by marketing programs and self-appointed gurus. In other words, time has not completely eradicated hope and determination in all of us. Despite ourselves, we do move forward - even if it resembles more a hobble than a jog. But at certain periods in the evolution of the human brain and psyche, moving forward isn't enough. Daring to change directions, veering away from the oncoming blinding headlights, can do wonders - even if that means rejuvenating old paths or opening up new roads where none have existed before. What has not changed over centuries is that parents, for the most part, care. We might not have the "right" answers all the time and we may search for solutions in the wrong places, but we still do love our children and we do want the best for them. And this is why this book is calling for (1) the questioning of things as they are and (2) the re-introduction of the tried and true technique of *encouragement*.

*Encouragement* has always been and remains to this day one of the mainstays which feeds the core of a family and a child's soul - rendering them strong and resilient - often, despite themselves. And though more sneers than appreciation are expressed regarding *encouragement*'s claims, its essence must be revisited if caring about our children has any true meaning.

## Too Plain To Be Beautiful

But the very idea of *encouragement* is more often than not considered too plain to be appreciated. We can't seem to wrap our minds around it. Is it too simplistic? Are the times as anxiety prone, tension-filled and destructive as stated? To the first question, I say no.

To the second, yes. Children are like the proverbial mine canaries. If not only a few, but many appear unwell or distraught, there really is a problem. And the "canary children" do sense problems in our environment. They may not be able to define or describe their situation intellectually but they "know" deep down in their gut whether things are OK or not. And in our contemporary social context things are not well. Another powerful bellwether is defined by our bizarre adult need to now see life as a series of symptoms and syndromes - diseases - anomalies to be dealt with - problems in need of chemical realignment. Our children's caged energies are no longer perceived as wondrous strengths anymore. They are seen as uncontrolled exuberance, over-excited self-expressions, attention deficits and nail biting despondency. But rather than look around us, to hone in on the situation which might be the cause of our defective perceptions, we too often focus on children and childhood as the culprits. We see them, their behaviours, as the "in need of change" elements in any and all contexts.

Children rarely adapt well to disturbed environments. Their reactions are therefore a healthy response to what is not good for them. What is not healthy, is an environment which forces them into these specific reactions and behaviours. We don't seem to see the correlation between the crazy times and the anxieties of our children. And because we don't, pharmaceutical interests are more than willing to "help us deal" with it all. . .

Through television, newspaper and magazine ads we are constantly reminded that "life is a bitch". BUT lucky for us, there are "easy" solutions. "Just ask your doctor. . ." By repeatedly being promoted-to about what ails us - we eventually get it. . . We begin to understand what we or our children "have". . . But then, we're also told that everything is OK. It's "normal to have such problems". . . Everybody has "it". And, naturally, there are solutions available to make things "go away". . . or at least provide us with more fun than we are having now by toning down or changing the symptoms.

If we are to believe advertisers, our lives have become nothing more than a series of situations to be taken care of. . . problems to be solved. . . usually easily. But the proposed solutions don't come cheap. . . Easy fixes are more often than not expensive and as they are not really solutions but rather pseudo-band-aids, the doses need to be repeated and repeated over and over.

## On Being Underwhelmed. . .

Annually, Americans spend billions on drugs. Actually we spend more on altering our moods than we do on education and the related arts. And In such an environment, where everyone is considered ill or in need, it eerily becomes harder and harder to determine who the real sufferers and victims are in our world. Actually, real victims suffer more now than they once did - simply because they are forced into hiding behind the much more aggressively needy pseudo-victims in our consuming societies.

By rendering everything homogenous, generic and "normal" we both lose the capacity to deal with anything on our own and we lose, in the shuffle, those people who actually do need recognition and assistance for the "real" emotional and mental difficulties which assail them. But then, there's no real money in dealing with such small numbers is there?

After awhile acceptance of what we are told "is" sinks in. It is so much easier to simply give in since we will be much happier, less miserable and much more in tune with life if we just take our "meds", enjoy our 3-times the health limit of sodium laced fast foods and spray away those god-awful germs that seem to be invading our homes and doing dastardly things to our children.

In 2008, $5 billion was spent by pharmaceutical companies on direct to consumer advertising. In the United States, an average adult is exposed to 100 minutes of television ads for every minute he or she spends seeing a doctor. Every child in North America views more than 40,000+ ads a year - ads extolling the virtues of every product imaginable. Increasingly, many of those subliminally powerful ads are not so subliminal. In 1983, advertisers spent $100 million on television advertising directed at children. In 2006 alone (according to a review by the US Federal Trade Commission) 44 major food and beverage marketers spent $1.6 billion to promote their products to children under 12 and adolescents ages 12 to 17. Overall more than $8 billion dollars a year are shamelessly directed at children for all manner of products.

Though the following information may be considered "old-hat" (based on our consideration that yesterday is old) it nonetheless serves to define the situation in which we and our children increasingly find ourselves. In 2006, the Official Journal of the

American Academy of Pediatrics issued a policy statement on Children, Adolescents and Advertising. The abstract states:

> *"Advertising is a pervasive influence on children and adolescents. Young people view more than 40000 ads per year on television alone and increasingly are being exposed to advertising on the Internet, in magazines, and in schools. This exposure may contribute significantly to childhood and adolescent obesity, poor nutrition, and cigarette and alcohol use."*

In essence, whatever sells well, markets itself to sell even more. Pharmaceuticals are a large player in this "thank god it's Friday", "let's make you feel good" environment. Even before we know we have them, drugs disguised as medication are available to deal with our deeply rooted anxieties, tensions, worries and fears. And if our children display signs or symptoms which "may" be disturbing to us (rarely to them), "solutions" are now always available (both for them and for the adults who "deal" with them). Never mind that in 60 every second television spot, up to 30 seconds are spent "swiftly" presenting the dastardly and even fatal side-effects associated with the use of these ever so scientifically researched "pacifiers".

The same process is followed for fast foods and other "necessary" products. All advertising, in times of anxiety, need only 2 things: *Premise and promise*. First and foremost comes the premise: i.e. "not using the product" creates a problem for us. Secondly, the promise. It assures us that we will once again be happy if we are smart - i.e. if we use the promoted item. Naturally, the promotions reassure us that this product is "good for us" - and that it is being offered, oh so generously by the manufacturer, to help us overcome our discomforts. Add to this marketing barrage a 24 hour a day news programming scenario (whose sole purpose it seems is to promote the concept of a world gone to hell in a hand-basket) and the "creation" of total anxiety as a "norm" is complete.

# BEYOND DISCOURAGEMENT – CREATIVITY

> *The world will see better days when there is less craving for the next new product and more appreciation for the process of creation which brought about the existence of that product. - 98*

## An Adult Perspective

Nonetheless, despite all the doom and gloom, parenting is something all couples consider at one point in time - if not actually undertake. But increasingly, that dream seems more nightmare than fairy-tale. Today, parenting too often displays as a difficult and thankless task rather than a creative time of sharing, nurturing and discovery. And, for whatever logical reason, in more and more young couples we see the "process" delayed. Why? Because it seems that children in contemporary lives represent "the end of fun times". So, let's wait, OK?

Naturally, it isn't until much later that we realise that time is "running out" and that "we should really do something about the situation"... But when the miracle day finally arrives, what do we begin doing? Do we daily sing the praises of our miracle child while observing in awe their never-ending evolution and conquests? No, we begin doing what everyone seems to be doing. We worry. We worry rather than admire. We wonder at how difficult "the whole thing is going to be" rather than be lulled by the baby's capacity to take in everything at the same time. We worry about the world our child is inheriting. We worry about our ability to parent. (Will Super Nanny have time to save us from our idiocies?) We worry about strangers, We worry about money, the best pre-school, the best kindergarten, the best elementary and secondary school. We worry about the future, security, jobs, taxes and making sure we leave enough money to our kids so that they, in the end, aren't saddled with the "problem" of burying us old codgers... But we can't worry too much about that last worry because we have to find it within our budget to pay for all the other worries: job, mortgage and life insurance, health, liability, accident, car and disability insurance... Have I forgotten any other worries?

What we seem to do the most of, today, is worry and the children, who finally come into the picture, know it all too well. In our contemporary world there seems to be no room for daring or adventurous forays into the unknown - since the unknown is, as we are constantly told, bad, frightening and dangerous. In this victimized new world there is less and less room for giggling and silliness and wondrous dreaming... Our contemporary world is an environment of what ifs...

> *"It's raining outside sweet heart... If we go on that walk you want so badly, you'll get wet. You might catch cold... You might even get the flu... pneumonia maybe... What if?"*

## Be Forewarned...

Let's face it though. We do come by our anxieties and fears honestly. No other continent in the world has as many non-profit (?) organizations and authorities (using our donated funds) to teach us about the whys and wherefores of hog-tying our children. In this era of hovering parenthood, over-protection is called caring and allowing your child to grow and experience life freely is called selfish neglect. If your child plays outside (OMG!) She'd better be wearing knee pads, elbow pads, shin pads, bike helmets and other assorted safety wear. Otherwise... There is also a matter of finger-printing, and possibly injecting sub-cutaneous gps/id chips - just in case...

# BEYOND DISCOURAGEMENT – CREATIVITY

There is also a matter of (didn't I just start a sentence with this?) tv ads and magazine articles constantly repeating themselves about the ever-present dangers in our communities, parks, schools, playgrounds, laneways and shopping centres. . . It seems that the only viable way children can roam "freely" these days is to have us tag along as their embarrassingly ever-present "best buds". . .

Sarcasm aside. Those of us who consider life wonderful and accept to let our children be children, should be forewarned. . . We of this category are a rare breed which must be eliminated. . . Displaying "slack" parenting techniques will bring about a good sneer and reprimand from other parents who "know better". And if our behaviours do not change, there may be room for being reported to the "authorities". But even if we can hide from those neighbours who are just waiting to report us, we and the kids are never really "free". There are always the ever-present seasonal and or regional warnings about sun, wind, snow, rain, sand, grass, falls, scratches and "ugh!" those incomparable GERMS!

Is it any wonder that, for a contemporary child, everyday life is basically problematic at best and depressingly frightening at worst? Actually, we're all damned if we do and damned if we don't. . . And so, taking a frightened-cum-therapeutic approach to everything is current practice. Being medicated in order to deal with "whatever" is becoming the norm simply because it's easier than having to deal with everything else.

## My Johnny Has More Symptoms Than Your Johnny

It is as if, in this day and age, we do not see being born as the beginning of an adventure but rather, from the very beginning, nothing more than a process of psychological and physiological deterioration. In essence, it is all a matter of discouraged rather than *encouraged* perception. Everything we are seems to now be defined as a series of treatable problems which can only be dealt with (not through traditional humanistic and medical diagnostic procedures, religious, family or community council or mentored intervention) but rather through a consistent barrage of *new and improved* medications, therapies and psychological interventions.

Never mind that we are sold that these "aids to well being" "may" only coat the symptoms. Never mind that many of the promoted drugs have recognized debilitating or even fatal side-effects. It seems we are willing to do "anything" to rid ourselves of the emotional annoyances which disturb our new and improved expectation of and need for total contentment.

So..................

Does all of the above mean we are actually on our way to hell and beyond? No. It simply means that, yes, we have created very difficult times for ourselves but, no, their effects are not impossible to overcome.

But, that still does not answer the questions of: How did we get here? How have we allowed ourselves to slide so far from balanced and sensible living practices? But more importantly, the main question is: How do we get out of this morass? Why is this question the most important? Because it does not go back to blame or to point a finger or to get answers that tomorrow will not satisfy us. This last question is mot important because it simply recognizes that if we just stand here looking backwards, we'll never move forward. But then, that doesn't mean we should not try to understand "the enemy".

## A Jaded Negativity

If *encouragement* has lost its solid positive aura, it isn't far-fetched to assume that its arch-enemy and equal and opposite "discouragement" is still around. If truth be told, this jaded negativity, this destroyer of exuberance and adventure, defiantly maintains a hold on us. And because it does, it affects how we perceive and deal with our lives and families. And how children respond to life's offerings is seriously dependent on how they have been led to them.

> *How we perceive life and living is a matter of the precepts laid down for us and which ,by extension, come to form the basis of our value system. - 98*

By its very nature discouragement is not a tool used by sadistic persons but rather one which is wielded by the sad and anxious. It is not something which attacks or maims but rather is a feeling which gradually overcomes those who use it and, eventually, those who are subjected to it. Its consistent use by those we trust eventually drains them and us of energy. And once discouragement has established its roots, its residual impact is so deeply entrenched it needs do nothing else. Its work is done. And at that stage, it simply slinks away in satisfaction, hiding silently in a dark corner - waiting to pounce on yet another unsuspecting individual.

> *As much as we consider the world a difficult and dangerous place for our children, what frightens them more is the fear they see in our eyes, the extreme weakness displayed in our indulgent "yes" - when an authoritative "no" would have been the correct response. We chill our children to the bone when they see in us the discouraged stares and lack of enthusiasm for anything which smacks of adventure and discovery. These are the frightening things a child cannot abide. - 05*

Now, recognizing discouragement is not as easy as you would suspect. It rarely exhibits itself as an aggressive slap, scream, kick or insult. More often than not it is subtle and, as such, it is as dangerous as a viper. Discouragement wears many disguises. It infiltrates parenting and teaching techniques and attitudes. It hides amidst over-protection and worry, anxiety and insecurity, tension and stress, fear, anger and worry. Discouragement is also the nefarious byproduct of tiredness and impatience. Taking advantage of our weaknesses, it offers itself up as a safe and easy alternative to the efforts required to deal with what ails us. It encourages us to take the easy way out, the pseudo-solutions to problems. In essence, discouragement is the grim reaper of the senses, the master of depression.

By the very fact that it is rarely discussed or debated, discouragement enjoys a position of sanctuary within the protected walls of home and school. It is entrenched in our neo-traditions. Unchecked, it is habit forming. And its greatest power lies in its pretence at being a protector of children. This masked face gives it full reign in the area of individual and collective sublimation of exuberance. It is victim-creating and has one goal: establishing in us all a false security in *sameness* - of homogenous thought and action. The ultimate goal? Render the spontaneity of individuality obsolete. To discouragement, going off on a tangent of individual creativity is dangerous - not generic enough to fit a democratic mould, not dependent enough on the status quo or the politically-correct modifiers which dictate how life "should" be lived. And "shoulds" cannot abide thoughts of a different order.

> *It is generally by the least creative person in a room that pleasurable musings are disturbed - dreams considered a waste of time, fluttering butterflies annoying moths to be swatted and gotten rid of as quickly as possible. - 01*

## The Danger of Thinking

The very idea of thinking differently upsets those who are insecure - meaning those who espouse discouragement. Doing things differently attracts derision when times are difficult - but then, what better time is there to consider change? Nonetheless, where children are concerned, the hue and cry of the times remain:

> *"It might be better if you didn't try that dear. . . You might be disappointed. It isn't what it seems. . . You know how you get when things don't work out. . . Why take a chance? You might fail.". . .*

So why do we allow ourselves to be pummelled by the manipulative bully that is discouragement? Actually, it's because we welcome it. It promises to simplify our complex lives. It calms our stresses and sedates our anxieties by helping us avoid facing difficult situations. It pretends to eliminate pain and suffering by giving us alternative attitudes, "sedating soothers" and behaviours which make life easier and less demanding - or so it seems. It promotes a *"rather safe than sorry"* life style wherein *others* (i.e. specialists and varied authorities, institutions and corporations) take over. They know much more than we do. And they do make much better decisions than we do... don't they?

## Discouragement And Invisibility

Discouragement is real. It is strong. It is a subtle controller of individuals, families and the larger community. Its quest is to render invisible, to homogenize, to eliminate unique identities - to stop forward movement. Encouragement caresses us while we build our strengths. Discouragement, on the other hand, strangles. It holds us back - until we are no more.

To be or not to be invisible... That is the question every parent must ask themselves - when it comes to not only themselves but more especially to their children. As adults we have become used to - and our economy even seems to thrive upon our being a totally integrated and invisible part of the whole. We are, each one of us, like ants on an ant hill - working, striving, reaching up but never out - always returning to the same core tunnels, doing the same work, seeing the same faces and doing the same things as all of the other ants, day in and day out. And that, or so it is said, is reassuring. But in reality, it simply maintains a colony's status quo. And that is not the same thing as security.

In the ant world, being different from your cohorts is not an option. The colony is everything. The survival of the community depends fully on the submission of ants to do their respective jobs. This is not to say that an individual ant doesn't have the wherewithal to get the job done in a different manner - if the usual way is blocked. No, ants are resourceful in the realization of their communal tasks and responsibilities. But if, in the running of their everyday lives, a few ants choose to stray, i.e. become creative for creativity's sake, all of the ants could suffer - and some if not all of the ants could die. Where ants are concerned, creativity as a divergence from the homogenous occurs exclusively to (1) achieve the goals of the particular ant's designated job which, in turn, (2) protects the colony's integrity.

Ant creativity has a collective calling whereas human creativity must diverge from an all encompassing communal consideration if it and the "colony" are to survive. The spiritual health of a human individual, within a community, must be maintained if that community wishes to remain healthy. And whereas each ant within a colony is intellectually and genetically entrenched in a caste environment - based on a clone-style modus operandi, human communities depend on their individual members to live communally but think uniquely.

Without creativity, without the encouragement of individuals to be creative, human communities suffer from the diminishing capacities of their individual members whose unique perceptions and talents eventually erode through lack of use. In the human world, as in the ant realm, communities are formed by like-minded individuals. BUT human societies survive, thrive and evolve only when the unique creative spirits of each member are allowed free (not licensed) reign within that collective environment. Healthy communities are never threatened by the creative elements in their midst as it is only through creativity that the evolving colonies, as a whole, stay mentally, emotionally, spiritually and physically healthy.

*Un-encouraged* creativity, on the other hand, is a recipe for individual and communal disasters. Creativity diminishes in strength and eventually disappears when there is no room in a society for a recognized and respected self-expression. In essence, if a community of like-minded individuals banned or failed to encourage creativity, the possibility of that society's long term survival would be compromised. This is so as the creative potential required for its survival would no longer be available to that community. In such a situation, there would be no one who would have the capability of thinking outside the box or of seeing things differently in order to bring about solutions to new or odd community problems AND/OR a collective's diminishing strengths.

> *The ability of a community to battle, to fend off threat of a physical emotional or mental nature, is proportionatel to the relative strengths of its individual members. No society is immune to threat and total destruction when individual egos within its membership are in a weakened state. - 00*

Creativity, therefore, is a crucial requirement if the world's communities, states and countries are to survive the onslaught of nature and/or man's own self-serving or destructive tendencies.

> *When the worst enemy of a community is itself, creativity is the real victim. And any and all enemies at the gate need do nothing but wait for the community's increasing vulnerability to show as time inflicts an ultimate demise. - 00*

But, acknowledging and taking on discouragement - i.e. turning it on its ear to reintegrate encouragement, isn't simply a question of generic change for change's sake. Encouragement has as much an individual mental, emotional, spiritual and artistic health component as it does a communal health component. As previously stated, if individuals in a community are less than they can be, the community as a whole suffers. It deteriorates and its soul gradually fades. Therefore eliminating discouragement and re-introducing encouragement must not only be an individual's project. It must increasingly become a collective enterprise whose specific goal is to take back that which is individually ours - that which belongs to our children and their futures - and that which enhances our communal way of life.

## The Power of Encouragement

Through encouragement, creativity has the power to sustain individual uniqueness rather than abandon it to a mere cloned existence - no matter the circumstance. It is always ongoing and forward thinking. It ignores the victim within us by blooming despite the aridity of self-absorption. It allows an individual to positively produce despite any and all impediments. And this is the greatness of encouraged creativity.

Though an individual adult or child may have one or more disabilities or come from a difficult or debilitating background - these are never enough to negate a person's uniqueness nor that person's capacity to create. Nothing can deny the unique person an individual stand or their place in the community. As stated in the previous chapter, creativity does not occur because of suffering but *despite* it. This is what gives creativity its higher calling. This is what makes individual passion heroic. And this is why creativity must be preserved and forever encouraged.

# BERNARD POULIN

> *Even a child perceived to have limited potential has more creative energy than most of us will ever hope to have after the age of thirteen - 02*

When a person is creative, they open their mind and heart to the clearly displayed possibilities before them - where possibilities, through the destructive nature of discouragement, were once invisible. Creativity is the stuff of courage and is born from within an individual's passions and abilities. Creativity is the stuff of heroism and excellence. It is not the stuff of victimhood. It is not the stuff of cloned sameness. Creativity recognizes the past but does not wallow in it. It ties its reigns to the present and daringly forges ahead, not backwards. And though creativity acknowledges the self it does not navel-gaze.

## Homogeneity vs Creativity

Now, the sameness of contemporary homogeneity is not the kind that was naïvely evident in the post-2nd world war period of *"striving to be like the Joneses"*. This century's craving is more intense. It is not focussed on *simply resembling* the Joneses in sophistication and style. Rather the new version of this phenomenon is a desperate one. It has much more to do with *"being"* the Joneses - denying one's individuality in order to become invisibly homogenous - i.e.

no longer capable of displaying any uniqueness or individual trait tagging us as different than the Joneses. And why become "everyone else"? Because it makes our existence easier – less painful.

> *It is only through a striving, working hard democracy, one which looks onward and upward - not inward - that the finest form of freedom of expression can exist. For a democracy - become easy, become homogenous - needs ever-increasing regulations and rules and laws to maintain its "oneness". And this is what destroys the very essence of creativity, of self expression, of democracy - not some foreign threatening source. - 04*

In essence, homogeneity is the new norm (*i.e. what there is the most of*). It is comfortable. It eliminates anxiety about whether we are being "correct" or not. As adults, we are advertised to about the "right" cars, trucks and boats, activities and food, dress and most especially "pain killers" and sedatives of every ilk - (to which we are prompted to form a brand allegiance). And being as everyone else believes this to be true. . . should we not abide by this communal conformity? It is as if, through the promoted objects of compensation, we will be more strongly defined as a collective of sage consumers and masters of our homogenous destiny.

> *Marketing has sold us on the illusion of strength while our gluttonous consumption of that illusion has made us weak. - 04*

Even adolescents, once proud of "being their own person" now seem unable to resist the pressures and submissive nature of collective consumer wants and needs. Today, teen alienation from family and the larger community is a different state of being. Rather than a temporary interlude, preceding the inevitable acceptance of maturity and responsibility, this new and improved adolescence extends itself well into the 20s, 30s and beyond. At best, one of the most endearing traits of this stage is its obsessive attachment to "little boy" style baseball caps and daddy-sized low-slung pants.

> *Actually, the above comment is not far-fetched. If a grown man dressed in baggy pants and ball cap stands 300 feet or so away from a viewer, it becomes difficult to tell whether we are seeing a 9 year old or an adult. Disproportion in attire "reformats" a visual experience as it alters the perception of the shape and proportion of the clothed person. In essence what we see is an illusion - or would dressing in this fashion be better defined as "wishful thinking?".*

Grown men in such garb calling each other "dude" seem to have no idea that what was cute at 5 is rather oafish at 20+ years old. At worst, this new dependent and entitled group, which thrives on a freedom to "be", is exactly what it prides itself in being: dependent and irresponsible

Ironically, today's mid-teen adolescents are not much different than young adults a generation older than themselves. Both carry over into their unencumbered "whatever" lives childhood entitlements and "appearances". Both segments are equally and increasingly conformist, submissive and repetitive in their *creative* attempts to be whatever it is that they are trying to be - and that is to be dependently independent and most especially NOT adult, not "old".

## The Birth of Discouragement

During the good old days (50s and 60s) adults and children were ignorant if not neglectful of life's dangers. The focus was on being free from the too recent war which had affected families and incomes. Building a new life was more important than spending too much time with our one too many exuberant children. Child-rearing was still too traditionally based to cause guilt or regrets about its successes or failures. No one even seemed to bother figuring out how the concept of 1.5 statistical children fit into our new suburban settings. And though the introduction of television was the great fascination that it was, the media had not yet linked entertainment to titillation - or yet played "boogey-man" with 24 hour a day news-programming.

Despite McCarthyism, obsessions with bomb shelters and other cold war anxieties, families were generally oblivious - happy to be alive and wishing it on everyone else. This short fantasy interlude lasted through the Korean war but the Vietnam struggles rekindled worries that we could not erase easily.

Today, we live lives which are totally opposite the naïve yet idyllic times of the early 50s. Actually, the pendulum has swung so far it has almost ripped itself from its hinges. Adults are far too focussed on the world's dangers and far too obsessed with feeling guilty about failing and spending time with their children. But the biggest difference between these 2 eras is obvious: the first was founded on hope and strength. This latest is built on fear and impotence fueled by a bravado of the few while the majority sedates worries.

Today, childhood is no longer "free". In essence, it is a shackled existence. And despite the almost incestuous intensity of "quality time" fixations and parental over-protection, children and parents seem to have little or no idea about who they individually are. Children don't even know how their parents spend their time or what they "do" on a daily basis. All they know is that their parents keep saying: "thank god it's Friday!"

> *If I never know what my mother or my father does, all the while I am squirrelled away at school, how am I to fully know myself. . . to know recognition and appreciation and the emulation necessary for my "self" to grow into adult contentment? - 77*

Once, children rode in their father's delivery vans. They met the people in other positions that their parents met. They did the marketing with their mothers. They knew the neighbours their parents knew. They had incite into the community in which they lived. They were also partners in the functioning of the family unit. Children were actually expected to clean out the cat's litter box, wash dishes, make their beds, run to the corner grocer for bread and milk and comb their hair and sew on buttons and help dress or calm down the baby. Children, were "useful" and "needed" around the house despite their sometimes pain in the bottom attitudes. They participated. And because of that children felt warm and united and loyal to their families. They were part of the success of a household, not its snob appeal. 5 year olds were once actually perceived as "capable". They could put their boots and coat and mitts on. They could gather eggs in the barn before breakfast. They were not seen as "unable".

Today, a 5 year old is more likely to need his mother to wash his face, blow his nose and hold his hand while he screams his objections to her entreaties - and that, from the kitchen to the bedroom to the bathroom, and embarrassingly for all, this "normal" behaviour even follows the family into public spaces. Today, children are simply expected to look good in their name-brand jeans even if all we get out of them is sulking and whining. We even consider the never-ending ballet, baseball, hockey, theatre, violin, swimming, diving, art and tennis lessons normal. This is how contemporary life defines encouragement. Stay busy and maybe we can get through this without too much thinking about it. We create a family life so scheduled and complex that the only possible result in both children and adults is constant exhaustion and frustration. And then (deep down inside) we adults get upset when the children are incapable of taking everything we do for them in stride. Why can't they simply understand that it's all about them? It's for their own good. It would be so nice if they would just be happy...

## The Good, the Bad and the ADHD

Even very small children feel the pressures imposed upon them to be 19th century "suitable children", i.e. those we have made up in our minds exist - rather than the real ones we have. Children quickly associate that submitting to how adults want them to be defines the difference between being good and being horrible - and there lies the difference between receiving love and having it revoked. With parents wishing and wanting one thing and children needing another the very idea that life can be unbearable becomes possible. Such pressures cause anxiety to rise ever higher. And high anxiety causes "antsy" repercussions in both adults and children.

But where children are concerned, behaviour patterns are of great interest - especially to pharmaceutical corporations and specialists. To highlight their importance, childhood behaviours are given fancy acronyms - which identify them as symptoms and syndromes - things to be "looked into and dealt with". And being as these behaviours seem common in children, the whole situation is perceived as a childhood "disease", an inability to cope, an unstoppable societal infection gone wild. Note: It is not new that children and the state of childhood are scape-goated. Reviewing adult perception of the past is quite informative.

## History Ignored, History Repeated

In Aristotle's time, children were the property of their fathers who could also decide whether they lived or died. In the Middle Ages (St-Augustin's time) they were perceived as weak but capable of being responsible by the age of 7. Basically an adult in the making (but). Their roles were indistinguishable from those of adults but their deaths or disappearance was nothing to write home about. With the Renaissance the concept of "equality" was introduced. Children were simply considered smaller adults. And though they were still the property of their fathers, the idea that they were more than simply chattel was considered in the 1529 educational treatise by Erasmus.

In the Classical period, some forms of child protection were introduced - as children were then perceived to be "reasonable" beings who were no longer property but rather vulnerable individuals in need of protection.

With Rousseau in 1762, "childhood" was presented as a specific time which must be respected and allowed as much freedom as its development required. Pushing a child to "become an adult too quickly" was introduced as not a positive consideration.

Freud introduced us to the fantasmagorical (his own?) inner life of infants. More reminiscent of 19th century erotic machination and paranoia than human dignity, his early 20th century "out damned spot" elucidations have yet to be put to rest.

Piaget, in the 1980s, has us focussing on the intelligent animal that we are rather than on the basal ogre Freud considered us to be. In essence, Piaget reports that children have unique reasoning capabilities which are poorly known by the likes of us. . . (adults, that is). Though no disciple of the child-centered mantra of the day, I do tend to go along with this theory.

To complete our short and informal foray into the history of children and childhood, it is important to note that not all evolution is progressive. . . . Therefore, I can only sum up by musing that, today, our perception of children is as "equals in the area of rights" more than in equality per se. I say this weird thing because children seem to be entitled more than they are allowed to be responsible. And as such, this state of affairs introduces us to the 21$^{st}$ century child as (l'enfant problême) - from the writings of Alain Renaut - i.e. "the problem child".

What is fascinating in all of this is that we did not in the past, and still have not today, looked at the context, the circumstances, the environment to see what is actually wrong. We simply say it is the children or childhood itself that is the problem. And because we are ignoring both the past evolution of childhood and the reality of childhood in the present we are in for a complex and problematic life with our children and a complex and problematic future with them as adults.

Children are perceived as problematic today because they seem to fight or run from "what is" And to children today, "what is" is not healthy. And if this child perception is correct, then their reactions and actions "are healthy" in that they cannot, as thinking and feeling individuals, abide that which might destroy them.

But then, adults also have difficulty facing "what is". They don't understand the reactions of their children to the environment. They don't associate their children's reactions to the reality of what is. They only see the misbehaviour, tantrums, anger and fear as "a problem in need of a fix". No one seems to realise that children are fighting for their lives.

Now, this "fighting" is more often than not perceived by adults (who are hell-bent on toning down the world to a level they can handle) as negative and therefore in need of "treatment". But in actual fact, the children who scream, yell and are belligerent are not the most seriously affected. It is those children who, having given up and given in - who "quietly" have no fight left in them, are the most discouraged. These are the ones who are down for the count.

## I Am Here... They Are There.

Discouragement is a root cause of the lack of creativity in children. But, in our era of easy and quick fixes, encouraging children to be the best can be is interpreted by many of us as being what "we expect them to be". Adults today (be they parents or teachers) consider that the problem between them and children is a lack of what we would consider a "calm response to rational request" ratio. And, par for the course, it is never our parenting or teaching techniques which are ever called into question when problems arise. In the end, the same conclusions are always drawn: children are (or have) the problem rather than are the victims of an environment lacking in encouragement. It is therefore not surprising that attention deficit disorder and hyperactivity connotations come so easily to the fore. What we can see, hear and be frustrated by, we more easily identify as problematic. What we fail to grasp is that a fighting kid is not a lost child. It's the one who gives up on trying to stay afloat who eventually drowns.

Since we live in a world which personalizes "everything" and since children are quick studies, they have learned from a very young age that it is not the solution that we need to find, when there is a problem but rather who must we please. And so they try hard and then harder - and because the air is filled with tension, their efforts are often thwarted. They then falter and "fail". And because failing today is personal , it is "failure". And this is when emotions erupt and situations get chaotic. So naturally, when we adults have no idea how to handle a situation, the children are the problem.

## Alice In Wonderland Riddles

Now, this negative theme of "I don't know what to do so let's nail the kid" is not new. But this new century seems committed to making it as bad as this concept can be.

Now, we know that when an environment is conducive to chaos, it is impossible for a child to make heads or tails of that chaos. And because of that, a child only does what a child can do - i.e. they react "normally" to an unhealthy situation. This has been true since time immemorial. But today, things are different. We don't just say that the problem is the child. When we face a disturbing child-adult situation, we place the total scenario at the feet of the child - proclaiming him or her "disturbed".

Since over the top behaviours due to over-the-top times don't register with what is considered "a normal reaction", we depend on quick and easy fixes which are so readily promoted to us by those who profit from offering us "a calm place" within our chaotic world. . . Today, when we can't deal with something, we know there are "fixes". The professionals tell us so. And so, we are taught to classify, categorize and diagnose our children with purported brain anomalies - disorders (which, only 30 or so years ago, never existed - and which even today cannot be and have never been proven legitimate).

> *More often than not, hyperactive children are more disturbing than disturbed. . . - 87*

Now, there have always been and always will be actual disturbance in the areas of individual personalities and behaviours - be they an adult's or a child's. There is no denying that some children and adolescents require professional help, including residential treatment in worst case scenarios. In all societies there are anomalies. And in caring societies these individuals are treated with empathy and professional expertise. That being said, it remains unreasonable to assume that so many of our children and adolescents are in need of a "chemical fix". It definitely is time for corporations, institutions, specialists in both educational and health systems (and adults in general), to stop staring at and "zapping" the "brats" in our midst. It is time to stop "fixing" and start taking a longer look in the mirror.

## The Inability Syndrome

Over and above ADD and the more inclusive ADHD disorders (amongst so many new and improved acronyms) we increasingly tack onto childhood behaviour and responses, there is an even older consideration which needs to be dealt with. From the XIXth century onward, we have come to treat children as more dependent. Rather than see children as teachable, we see them as less capable, less strong, less thinking as individuals and therefore more in need of being told what to do, and not to do. We find babies and infants and toddlers cute but "not much good at being anything else". We see young children as more incompetent and accident prone than older children and teens, and though we consider older children and teens semi-competent we still perceive older "child ages" to be obnoxious in their "deliberate" capacity to thwart us in our parental and teaching efforts.

In actual fact, the problem is not that children are incapable. The problem is that we see them that way. And from the time they are made to follow instructions - from the time they are old enough to obey and be directed - small children are made to feel (in equal and opposite intensity to their overall enthusiasm and wanting to help) too young, too small, too slow, too weak, or just not ready "yet".

Children, therefore, reluctantly but quickly adapt to a hierarchy of "inability". Discouragement meted out in constant proportions - by those who are essential to a child's need for love and nurture - are difficult to bear - but borne it must be. Even young children are aware that it is best to conform to adult perceptions - lest they lose out even more. Also, discouragement in a family environment is often based on the premise that time is of the essence. Things must get done quickly, efficiently and well: i.e. in an adult-like fashion". But most of all, things must be done "now!" And this leads to the "probability factor".

> *A well managed life is efficient.*
> *A well lived life rarely is. - 00*

## The Probability Factor

One of the more perplexing things in a child's life is the probability factor. It plays a large part in child discouragement. Right from the start it defines a child's role as 'less than", not up to par, not good enough, not old enough, not able. Based on unwritten adult rules, young children (because they are young children) are innately accident prone. It's not that significant adults consider young children totally inept but rather that - due to their age they can do less - much less than they actually can. Such a mind set on the part of adults causes an equally disturbing mind set in children. They want to grow up - but sadly, not because they wish to "be like" or to emulate their parents, teachers or mentors. No, wanting to be grown-up has less to do with hopes and dreams than it has to do with no longer wanting to be children. Being an adult is better to them because it is perceived as being free from *discouraging* remarks and directives. It means finally getting out from under - no longer being in the subordinate position of a lesser state of existence.

Now, by the age of 4, children are highly capable of participating in many *adult and family* activities. They are, for example, able to help clear a table after dinner, capable of drying dishes, sorting and putting pots and pans away and sorting and putting away folded clothes. Yet, too often the focus of attention is directed to the perceived *accident-proneness* of all typical 3 and 4 year olds - or the dangers involved in allowing a "poor little one" to be of any *use* to the family. Individual ability or talents or the desire to "be a part of" are overlooked since, statistically, it is believed that one toddler + one considered adult activity = imminent disaster.

If perchance an accident occurs, all possible contributing factors (poorly laid rugs, being pushed by an adult to hurry, being nagged to be careful, being teased by an older sibling or simply being excited at finally being allowed to participate) are never taken into account. When an accident occurs, all eyes freeze on the *culprit* who did this horrible *wrong*. It is no wonder that children associate accidents as nothing more than being bad and inability as being stupid or inept. Everything a little child does is perceived in the context of being either "bad" or "good". In other words - everything is personal. Nothing is ever objective. And after an incident (of the nature described above) comments inevitably ring out, which resemble the following:

## BEYOND DISCOURAGEMENT – CREATIVITY

> *"I knew it!" - "I told you, so!" - "I knew I'd have to clean up 'your' mess!" - "You're too small! Go play with your toys!"*

To a child these comments read as: *you are too weak, too young, too clumsy, too bad to be of any good.* Saturated with guilt - remorseful at ever having considered himself good enough, our 4 year old hero can do nothing more than pout off into the sunset. . . *discouraged* from ever trying again. But isn't it odd! We would never react this way if the person having an "accident" is an adult. . .

Example: Aunt Minnie is visiting. She stays for dinner. After the meal, she helps clear the dishes. With a few-too-many drinks under her belt, Minnie teeters. She drops and breaks a favourite tea cup. How solicitous we become. . . how forgiving. . . how supportive. . . how sensitive to her shame, how warm and caring we are. We would never remind her that she has had too much to drink. More often than not we make silly excuses - trivializing the situation - i.e. *making her feel loved.*

Our generous and respectful comments sound like the following:

> *"Don't worry dear, it was already chipped"* or *"I was going to throw it out, anyway"* or *"I never really did like that cup"* - (forgetting that it was a gift from Aunt Minnie, herself). . .

No, we would never discourage an adult. . .

*Discouragement is for children and old folks. - 99*

Another factor to consider is the cumulative effect of discouragement. The more a person (of any age) is discouraged, the more they become anxious and accident prone. The more they become victims, dependent on others to make decisions for them and fearful rather than adventurous when it comes to testing the unknown. When we render personal that which is not, the consequences are inevitably negative.

## The Curse of Personalizing

The reason we think children "incapable" is strangely related to our own inability to separate being good from doing well. And often this habit translates into an attitude of regimented efficiency which in and of itself makes accidents inevitable. Efficiency is always associated with adult impatience and the ever present "right way" to do things and the inevitable. . . doing things "right away". Rarely do our reasons for discouraging a child's participation have anything to do with their true abilities. This is not to deny that accidents where children are concerned will not occur or denying that children do have less developed abilities. Rather, it is a question of being more realistic in the area of expectations and responsibilities. But then, the perception we have of our own creative abilities is often at the root of how we treat children in the areas of self- expression and individuality.

To be creative, a person must feel free to discover and analyse why things work or don't work out. Errors as well as successes in any undertaking must be perceived as partners in the learning and discovery processes. Both experiences are stepping stones to further exploration and discovery. But in our perfectionist society "error" is not only viewed as an everyday failing, it is viewed as a "moral" failing - a fault in a child or adult's make-up. This attitude causes children to fear trying, to fear change, to refrain from implementing any new course of action or even thinking. In such situations, children learn to avoid anything which even remotely resembles the unknown.

To risk exploring on one's own means tempting fate. To a secure person, this is exciting. To an insecure individual this means the possibility of facing rejection due to an "expected" loss of face. After awhile, to a child, the possibility of failing is too much to handle and the individual so attacked succumbs to the feeling that their ineptitude is part of who they are.

## Perfection vs Excellence

The oft repeated "Oh, I can't even draw a straight line!" is a case in point. The erroneous perception, that only perfection (a "straight" line) is acceptable, is always preceded by a mind set which rules out error or trial as normal. This one sentence says more about so-called self esteem than does artistic or creative ability.

The key word is "straight" - not curved, jagged or playful. . . but STRAIGHT! Etymologically speaking, the word "straight" deserves a closer look. It means: going in one direction, following a narrow, predetermined and measured course. No deviations are permitted since the line would no longer be straight.

The French word for straight (droit or droite) defines more clearly the censorship power of this word. The definitions are revealing: (Droit(e) = correct, "right", just, acceptable, good, moral, dependable, reliable, conservative, non-threatening and. . . uhm . . . "perfect".

Admitting that we are not able to draw a straight line subliminally implies that we think of ourselves as LESS than perfect, less than those who are able to do this. This is an admission to the world that we are not as "good" as we would want to be seen to be. We are stating, through a generic phrase, that we feel incompetent to do what is universally accepted as a good or "right" thing to do, i.e. draw a STRAIGHT line. Forget that this accomplishment is quasi-impossible to achieve.

Failure to achieve in our society is closely linked to "failing as a human being". Failing to succeed at anything is related to our universally false consideration that, in our lives, perfection is what must be sought. We don't perceive perfection as an ideal but rather an achievable trait. We fail to accept that this quest is an impossibility - a fantasy of incredible proportion.

Excellence, on the other hand, is the equal and opposite of perfection. It *is* achievable. And it is so because it does not impose a moral component on its realization. Excellence has nothing to do with who or what we are. It deals exclusively in how well, and in what unique way, an individual is able to accomplish something at any particular moment in time.

The seeking of perfection inevitably causes failure and feelings of inadequacy in both adults and children. It leads to feelings of *"I'm not good enough"*. And since we have failed in the past, and we have suffered the resultant shame and humiliation through transgression from the "straight and narrow", WE GIVE UP. . . We won't try again. . . "It hurts too much!" The long slide down to a level of "just getting by" - and for some, depressive mediocrity - begins here. The fear (guilt), which causes us to stop trying, to stop creating a new world for ourselves, is at the root of discouragement. It leads to a *"Thank god it's Friday"* mentality which gives our work a status of penance for living an "ordinary" or just so-so existence, rather than an opportunity to shine as a creative individual.

In such a world, self-expression fades. When the child in us can do nothing more than struggle to regurgitate only what we have been taught is correct and acceptable, life slowly becomes discouraging. The ability to experiment, to explore, to discover and to present our findings is easily stunted when we are not encouraged. As children memorize mannerisms, attitudes, behaviours and expressions (for the purpose of avoiding getting into trouble) creativity is nipped in the bud.

On the other hand, encouraged children take on mannerisms and positive behaviours easily for no better reason than that it feels good. And for that to be, the relationship between significant adults and children must be a mutually positive one.

Now, this does not mean that adults must "cowtow" to children's demands or feelings of entitlement. Adult guidance, authority and experience should not be belittled or shunted aside. They are important ingredients in the preparation of children for independence. But, sometimes our need to "be the adult" interferes with a growing up process. Even in areas where children are the "more competent", they are often made to feel inferior.

Example: A child is drawing a picture. A nearby adult feels the intensity of the child's concentration and interprets the situation as being "too difficult for the child to handle". The adult then interrupts the child in order to "make things easier", saying: "No, no, dear. . . That's not how "WE" draw a house! Let Mommy, Daddy, aunty show you how. . ." Again, the perception that children concentrating equals a child suffering is frightening to a contemporary adult, hellbent on protecting their child from everything which might upset them. Adults who feel that children should always "appear" happy and carefree are deluding themselves and imposing upon children their own life frustrations. Telling a child that we believe him or her to be untrained and therefore incompetent (i.e. in need of adult help) is a too prevalent practice to be ignored as a source for eliminating creative potential.

> *By "colouring within the lines" I was compensated with acceptance. - 81*

In areas of play, where children have no creative equals, adults are often unable to control themselves. They seem to have an insatiable need to "structure" everything which appears too random, undisciplined or free. Children, on the other hand, have no problems making, altering or "dumping" rules as they go along.

As a 4 or 5 year old, have we not felt a twinge of frustration , a pinch of discouragement, at the constant adult intervention in "our" games? Have we not experienced the incessant need of adults to impose their need for "quality time"? How often, when drawing or painting, are we asked: "What's that?!" To us, the "offending" artwork is an eloquent rendering of our perceptions and/or interests, or simply a laying down of beautiful colours or shapes. Yet, as often as not, we are given the benefit of the "expertise" of those who so persistently proclaim: "I can't even draw a straight line. . ."

From the time we are very young, our captivated, curious and perceptive minds are gradually taught that until we are "older" others will do, see, arrange, plan and organize for us. . . (We simply aren't able, "yet", to fill in the lines neatly enough. . .) Very young, we are lulled into believing that trials and errors of any kind are stressful, wrong and - mostly - a sign that we are "not good at" what we are doing. Whether it be about drawing, dressing, eating, walking, sitting, talking, smiling - childhood stress can be avoided. . . if only we would listen to those who "know better".

Most of us were raised to think that there is an EASIER (i.e. BETTER) way of doing things - (since errors are bad, not good, not right. . . not straight and. . . not certainly fast enough). How quickly we learned that someone out there, bigger, stronger,

## BEYOND DISCOURAGEMENT – CREATIVITY

brighter, more aware, and more experienced than we, had all the "right" answers... In essence, that is what contemporary life is all about - the need to harmonize everything into a homogenous therapeutic jelly in which we all float without stress.

Now for a society to succeed, it is obvious that homogeneity of values is necessary. Survival of the whole depends on a disciplined and well organized grouping of similarly visioned peoples. Yet, in the quest for harmony, societies must not fall into the trap of sameness to the point of stagnation and self-destruction.

> *Without the "mind's eye", truth becomes absolute, facts infallible, creativity impossible, innovation obsolete, discovery implausible and stagnation inevitable. - 97*

Stagnation is the cause of the eventual eroding of democratic foundations - be they anywhere on this planet. And self-destruction is the fate of any society which can only find its security through the sublimation and elimination of individual creative potential.

As has been stated before, the need to express one's individuality is vital. It is not detrimental to a democratic society. And this need to self-express must be nurtured from birth; not stifled. Even in areas of supposed non-importance, such as infant scribbles and 3 year old attempts at choosing and matching clothes, children must feel that their attempts are not objectionable. Self-stimulating activities are all part of the process of defining and refining uniqueness. The answer to a happy child is rarely more complicated than that?

In essence, the family is a society in miniature. A child is a citizen of that community and parents are the prominent political and judicial figures. They formulate the laws and regulations which permit that this society survives through thick and thin. When a family functions adequately, the citizens are happy and thrive both as individual members and as a collective. When it does not, the community members suffer and so does the society.

> *The ultimate family unit is a safe haven, in which each member is uniquely creative and each is a collaborative partner in the collective well-being of the whole. - 77*

How a child survives family life determines how they enter into and participate (or not), as older teens and adults, in the larger society. If we teach our children to be submissive and/or aggressive, that is how they will deal with the community and the world they inherit. How else would they be?

> *How you were taught to analyse situations as a child determines how you handle life as an adult. - 83*

# BEYOND DISCOURAGEMENT – CREATIVITY

Sharing - Graphite - 6" x 3"

*Creativity does not exist without difficulties and most of all eccentricity. When it doe,s it is not creativity. And without creativity, there is no passion and without that - no life. And this is why homogenization in races and cultures, governments and the arts is the devastating virus that it is. To generically render ourselves safe in the bosom of sameness is to sit back - to await the only thing it is possible to create in such an environment: extinction. - 95*

BERNARD POULIN

## The Last Stronghold

In our societies, we no longer profit from the "it takes a village to raise a child" concept. The only other recognized significant adults in children's lives (other than parents) are teachers. But despite their best intentions, these professionals now see themselves forced into positions their professional standing has never prepared them for. Once, teachers focussed on preparing the minds and hearts of children for the future. But today, children come from a variety of backgrounds and families, struggling to keep their heads above water in expensive and dysfunctional times. Children start school much less disciplined than they once were. They are less independent, more demanding, less self-assured, more anxious and more disconnected. And so, teachers constantly adapt themselves and their roles to meet an ever more demanding position, client-base and assorted family configurations. At one time, the teaching profession was respected. It was ruled by a passionate enjoyment of seeing children thrive and grow. Today, it seems that those who teach have little time to focus on children as too much time is taken up with requisite bureaucratic directions, parental demands and never-ending political storms controlling the direction schools must go. Somewhere in between, children are considered. . . but the results do not do justice to what the children are capable of offering. Today, teachers must be parents, foster-parents, social workers, grandparents and confidantes - and all without being able to get close enough to actually comfort and advise.

And with the demand that higher and higher degrees define what is or is not a good teacher, the work academics are mandated to do will have to align itself more and more with the concept of efficiency and less and less with individual student needs. Naturally, the more statistical and bureaucratic, the less personal an academic milieu becomes. With the idea of merit pay added to the fray, results oriented schools will be created to meet the increasing "success" rate demands. And because of this, the very idea of excellence will be abandoned. Less and less will be required of students in order to achieve the goals upon which budgets and political recognition depend. And as more and more children fail to achieve what normally would be required, more and more will pass because it is mandated that they do.

Nonetheless, the academic milieu is the last creative-outlet refuge children have in our discouraged world. And yet, this purportedly sophisticated learning environment has been forced to reconfigure itself over the past 100 years to take on larger and larger numbers of children within fewer and fewer fenced-in, separated from the community, warehousing systems.

While decrying the inhuman proportions of orphanages and work-house style institutions of past centuries, we've seen fit to eliminate the more human dimensions of local schools in order to run cheaper and more "cost-effective" big-box enterprises. And this, under the guise that smaller local environments do not provide adequate facilities and equipment required in the pursuit of contemporary education. From these constantly evolving plans and re-plans, fiscally efficient authorities promise a greater variety of "products" while assuring that in the larger "new and improved" facilities a generic sameness, a homogenous output, will be the prize they allocate to children and families at the end of the school year. Never mind that promises made are weak and the results even weaker. No solutions to this present state of affairs is in the offing (whether in the near or even far future). And that is because the evidence of children learning less and less and being less and less prepared for the world are not seen by decision makers as "immediate priorities".

The question we should ask ourselves is the following: If children are becoming less and less intellectually and emotionally functional, how long will it take before someone actually recognizes the drastic situation our nations are in - and chooses to do something about it?

Michael LeGault in his recent book *"Think"* quotes John Bardi, a lecturer at Penn State: *"Today's students. . . lack the critical thinking skills for higher learning".* He wasn't talking only about college and university students. And he wasn't denying that contemporary children and adolescents are intelligent.

That young people today are more aware of a lot of things is undeniable. That they are incapable of analyzing and assimilating even a minute portion of the content of their analysis is also undeniable. That our children are behind in their ability to function at almost all grade levels (compared to children in most other countries) is a testament to the dysfunctional capacities of our systems. Nonetheless, the idea is not to sit back and complain. The only way to handle this situation is exactly to "do" something. But, are we there yet?

> *A heavy dose of lowest common denominator stimulation does not constitute a more informed mind, substantive thought or a more caring viewpoint. It simply makes what we know"user friendly". - 01*

Our children are not "dumber"than any other. They are simply numb, bored, anxious and forcibly distracted by the "take me away from it all" inventions we give them to keep them quiet and out of our hair. By alienating them from the ability to reason, to feel, to create, to respect, to heed, to lead we deny them a future of independence and freedom. How we reverse this diseased trend depends on how and when we decide to react to the very reality of this conundrum we face.

## BEYOND DISCOURAGEMENT – CREATIVITY

And so, having reviewed the conundrum and the context in which it was born - (i.e. the environment in which our children are presently trying to keep their heads above water) it is time to take stock of where we are and where we all are going. Our decline is a reflection of the lowest common denominator sameness we have come to accept as normal and healthy. Present trends, therefore, need to be reversed. Excellence has to be re-introduced into our lives - as a goal to be reached for on an individual and collective basis. The possibility to be as creative as each of our children can be must be enhanced. And for that to be, encouragement must be part and parcel of the environment we offer children. But are we ready to embrace this? Is encouragement possible in this era of "uber" me, myself and I? Encouragement and creativity are not that far from our core desires. Creating an environment in which our children can soar is not that difficult. It simply demands that we free ourselves to be encouraging and free our children to shoot for the stars. But until then, the battle continues. . .

The following are samples of headlines and quotes from newspapers during a 6 month period in the past year:

- **"Dangerous" Inactivity Puts Children At Risk** Active Healthy Kids Canada report blames computers, TV time as major offenders. "If we don't deal with this now, we are going to mortgage our children's futures." - Kelly Murumets, CEO, Participaction.

- **Meltdowns Or Mental Illness?** In 2005, 376,460 children in Canada (to the age of 12 years) were prescribed atypical anti-psychotic drugs. In 2009, that number was 994,002. In 2005, 257,605 teens between 13 and 19 were prescribed atypical anti-psychotic drugs. In 2009, that number was 691,237.

- **The Temper Tantrum May Be The Next Childhood Mental Disorder** Temper dysregulation disorder (TDD) will be the new ADD if the Diagnostic And Statistical Manual of Mental Disorders has its way. This psychiatrists bible is undergoing a first revision in 16 years. . . And so it seems that both the helping professions and the pharmaceutical companies are in for a new era of "latest and greatest" disorders. . . Christopher Lane, author of Shyness: How Normal Behavior Became A Sickness, states that for the most part "tantrums are a healthy expression of frustration". But then, isn't that what creating a new illness is all about - quieting. . . sedating those who would dare react against "the status quo" i.e. what is abnormal and unhealthy?

Here are a few more headlines:

- **Canada's Kids Get an F For (Un)fitness** It seems that only 1 in 8 schoolchildren do the recommended 90 minutes a day of physical activity. None of the provinces and territories of the country are meeting the Canadian physical activity guideline. 88% of Canadian children are either well on their way to being unhealthy, are already overweight or are obese.
- **The New Normal: Paranoia**
- **Reflections Of A Failing System**
- **Accused Bullies Sue Over Extreme Punishment**
- **Smother-Love? No, Just Doing My Job**
- **Is Having A Disorder The New Normal?**
- **Fat Nation - Heavier, Wider, Weaker**

## BEYOND DISCOURAGEMENT – CREATIVITY

- **Doctors Being Paid Top Push Drug Study**
- **Doctors Expecting Surge In Canadian Obesity Rates (in both children and adults)**
- **Someone Hurt Your Feelings? Try Tylenol**
- **Sedentary Students Report Poorer Health**
- **(TV) Contestants So Dumb They're Hilarious**

Everyday, my comments seem to be vindicated - or at least corroborated. And that doesn't so much make me grin as it makes me sad. In all that I have written in the past pages, I sincerely wish I was wrong.

And so... We are back to square one in this context of conundrums... Why? And... And how serious must it get before someone does something about it?

> *What is most wondrous about life is that once an answer to a question is found there is always another more fascinating or more frightening question to be asked. For it is when there will be no more questions to be asked, no situations to be pondered and no answers to be submitted, that life as we know it will cease to be. - 02*

# 3
## The Key

The Portrait Artist - Oil – 2004

*The illiterate of the 21st century will not be those who cannot read and write, but those who cannot learn, unlearn and relearn. - Alvin Toffler*

## You're Not The Boss Of Me!

Providing and maintaining an environment worthy of children's needs and creative potential is the role of parents, teachers and mentors. Children need to feel that the guardians of their world are not there to stunt emotional and physical potential through excessive safety measures or controlling attitudes which limit potential. *Encouragement,* as the root base of environment, *must be felt to be there* by children. And oddly enough, *that encouragement* involves saying no, no and no again, if and when required during a child's growing years. A positive environment is not one in which children run roughshod over anyone and everyone in their path anymore than happiness is a permanent and total state of complete contentment. It is not a time and place where significant adults give up their parental authority to child-centred obsessions either. Rather it is an atmosphere in which children, in their wild abandon to discover the world and test parameters, feel protected from situations which may cause serious loss and/or damage to themselves or to others. In essence, to feel secure, children need to know that their parents are there being parents - not chums or "buddies". How else can they feel truly safe?

Now, if that means that we parents, teachers or mentors get our feelings hurt when children say they "hate us" because we exercise authority (i.e. when we are being who we are supposed to be) I think the appropriate phrase for that is: *suck it up!*

> *You can't expect a 9 year old to do as he is told when during all the previous years of his life he has been telling his parents and teachers what to do. - 82*

Children go on the attack, or manipulate their environment, for 2 reasons:

1. To test it for leaks and loopholes and
2. When that environment lacks in the areas of structure and self-confidence.

Children need security. They want someone in charge - even if that means doing the job themselves. And children when they are allowed to, or feel a need to be, can be class "A" manipulators and controllers. So, if we want them to play the role to which they were born it's up to us to play ours. If at worst, children have reached a lowest common denominator level as whiners and criers it's time to take a good look at ourselves before yelling at them. An environment which opens the door to negative behaviour is one which must be adjusted if a child is ever to feel secure enough to tone down the "I'm not feeling good about this place" rhetoric. So, when do children act in this "impossible way"? I can only answer that in unsweetened, un-candy-coated terms... Children are a constant pain in the posterior when the environment is more conducive to discouragement than *encouragement*.

## The Key

Now, I can go on and on about who's in charge of a child's life... But that's not what this book is about - (though my whole premise is based on not being afraid to take back parental authority). Whatever the argument, parenting's main role is not about control, discipline or domination. It is about *encouragement*. And it can never be said enough that:

> *Encouragement is the key requirement upon which mental and emotional health, along with creativity, flourish.*

Without it children are left in limbo - unknowing, afraid, anxious about and stymied by the lack of a secure and stimulating atmosphere. Without *encouragement*, children "feel required" to substantiate their parent's personality rather than develop their own. A healthy child's persona gradually develops from birth. When it doesn't, or for some reason it is stifled in its process of becoming, that child's identity is well on its way to not being "anybody" let alone becoming anything.

Children need an arena conducive to their own sense of being, their own sense of curiosity, adventure and discovery - not someone else's. They need a nod of recognition and support which gives them permission to fly - along with the safety net only a responsible "adult" can provide. But how does *encouragement* fit into an average family's life? How do encouragement, environment and creativity relate? What, in concrete practical terms, is *encouragement*? If an environment conducive to *creativity* is crucial, what essential part must adults play in accompanying their children in this exploration, discovery and savouring of the world? But how can parents do more? They are already overwhelmed!

## The "What" Of It

E*ncouragement* isn't a complicated premise. It doesn't need a book rules or directions. It isn't an "add-on" or a special skill. Encouragement is what we do naturally for those we care about and feel an adult responsibility for. To encourage simply requires that parents, teachers and mentors be comfortable in their own skins. And this means being relaxed about the whole concept of providing the security zone within which a child can grow without hesitation or anxiety. Now, I am not saying that *encouragement* is a new-age - "all is right with the world" feeling. *Encouragement* is rather more important than that. It is more the foundation of an environment than its aura. It allows that when things go wrong, there is an "equal and opposite" feeling that with a bit of thought and determination things can still go right. It is the sense that in one's home, school and community "everything's OK" - not because the world is perfect but rather because it is flexible and "forgiving".

Now, this is certainly not a psychological or therapeutic definition. And it definitely fails in the area of professional jargon. But *encouragement* can't be defined or codified in rule-based or formulaic terms. If anything, *encouragement* is the result of personal feelings of responsibility and affection proudly displayed by significant adults who then direct those feelings towards the present and future well-being of a child.

If anything, a truly encouraged child is one who eventually becomes less and less dependent - without ever completely abandoning the need for at least a "smidgen" of it.

*Encouragement* comes to reside calmly within a person. In time, it is so ingrained in an individual's psyche that it becomes the driving-force, leading that individual to become their own natural encourager - along with sharing that feeling with others. Encouragement is a more digestible concept if we first and foremost look at it not as a concrete something but rather as a something "sensed". Children may not necessarily understand what happens to them but they do "sense" it. They feel it through their pores - much like knowing you are loved even if and when times are tough. And this is so because *encouragement* is not something which runs away during difficult times. Actually, once it becomes a part of our lives, encouragement resists leaving. It holds fast and feeds the inner strengths required to overcome difficulties - both in adults and children. And the more confidence and strength and hope a child gets over time, the stronger that child becomes because of this *encouragement* diet.

Now, sometimes I think my need to want everyone to know *encouragement* is so great that I end up trying too hard to explain it…Its lack of physicality is a serious problem. If it was a more tangible "thing", explaining it would be easier. But hopefully, through more concrete, down to earth examples, I will be able to describe more clearly just how powerful yet how simple this basic life element really is.

## In The Beginning… The Key

For *encouragement* to be at its most potent within the self, its impact must begin to be felt from the time of childhood and adolescence. Again - from the very beginning, a child needs nothing but the self and an encouraging environment to grow. It thrives on discovery and the pleasure discovery gives it. But as the baby grows, and as it integrates with and is integrated by others, the need to be connected vies with the need to discover and create. And because of this combination of (and competition with) connection, the only way a child can return comfortably to its creativity roots is through the encouragement of significant others - the very same others who took the child "away from themselves" in the very beginning. *Encouragement,* coming from this group, is crucial. It confirms with the child that all is well - that it is OK to be connected intermittently with others and yet still go off to be oneself - to be who we are, to think the way we think, to be creative and to be excited about other things than what the world tells us we should want and think. It is a given that, as they grow, children need to strike out on their own - to be stimulated by their very own imagination and wonder. *Encouragement* from those who care is *key* to burgeoning childhood adventure. It is vital because it neither leads nor follows. When implemented, encouragement simply IS at the service of the individual.

# BEYOND DISCOURAGEMENT – CREATIVITY

As stated previously, children need nothing to get their sensual and mental juices flowing - except the freedom to do so. Now in this chapter an array of attitudes, environments, behaviours and atmospheres is outlined. The suggestions are not offered as specific solutions to generic problems. Rather, they are ideas geared to stimulating questions about what would be most encouraging in each of our own unique home and school environments. All comments, anecdotes and suggestions are samples of, sources for, or results of *encouragement*.

This chapter's job is to simply open the door wider to the array of possibilities from which encouragement stems. Its goal is to revitalize the uniqueness of every family constellation and eliminate, in the process, the possibility that destructive homogenous existence impose itself upon our homes and classrooms.

Once again, the following descriptions, suggestions, comments and anecdotes are not part of a doctoral thesis on child rearing techniques. Nor do they pretend to be. Rather, they focus on the potential consequences of *encouragement* - the concept that life is only impossibly complex when no solutions to problems are foreseeable, anticipated or even considered.

As parents, the best that we can offer is the best of ourselves. Our role is to encourage children to dare, to hope, to go out boldly into the world and to accomplish the best that they can be and. . . in turn, get back from the world the best that it has to offer.

If we start at the beginning, calmly and lovingly resolute, our children will follow our lead - and do the same with their children. For within every child is a burgeoning excitement for life and its riches. And within every child's environment there is the potential to either *be encouraging* or to be *discouraging*. And because that is so, our children are faced with 2 possibilities: learn to encourage themselves and others or discourage and be discouraged.

> *Wisdom comes peacefully not aggressively, speaks softly not angrily and creates daringly not submissively. - 07*

## The Times And How We Live Them

We live in the 21<sup>st</sup> century - with all of its demands, tensions and bizarre foibles which tend to foster stress. And yet, within this chaotic environment, I promote *encouragement* - positive thinking. Could this essay be nothing more than a naïve belief in a "nothing's impossible" and an "everything is rosy" mind set? I doubt it. . . I have spent much of the past 4 decades observing adults and children alike - trying to figure out what makes them happy or sad, eager or discouraged, connected or disconnected. And every child I have seen grow to be strong, resolute, brave, compassionate and sensitive has been a child nurtured on *encouragement*.

> *To be truly alive is to create, to judge no one, to live judiciously and to be free of domination. - 92*

This is not to say that individuals raised on hope and courage are totally free of trouble, problems or illness. On the contrary, life at times can be a challenge. But, what *encouragement* does is give each human being the power to deal with situations, to face them head-on. An encouraged individual is one who does not become submissive, weakened or destroyed by the weight of negativity and anxiety.

That is a legacy we owe our children - the strength to be free and proudly independent - despite what negativity might throw at us.

# BEYOND DISCOURAGEMENT – CREATIVITY

But in our quest to render the world in which we live "more livable", more encouraging, we must be patient. We adults have been evolving in very discouraging times -we are not the most prepared to deal aggressively with a definitive change in our support patterns. By the time we are in parenting mode, our generation has been carrying around the results of both good and bad training for quite a while. Constantly changing pop-psychology attitudes and behaviors and pseudo-guru values has done its damage to our ability to "think on our own". It is as if we have been taught drawing and painting by an incompetent art teacher who had us believe in all the wrong things. And, once sent out to fly on our own, we discover the teacher gone and our coping skills lacking. Bad habits, therefore, need to be unlearned before we can take on the mantle of self-worth. Simply stated, putting *encouragement* into play means getting rid of that which no longer applies - and actually never did.

But be careful. Our children know who we are. They will tend to look warily upon this "new person" we are becoming. Taking it slowly and calmly is the best scenario. Though mentoring our child is not rocket science - it nonetheless is not a done deal - just because we suddenly decide that this is the way to go. (I only have to remember the darting looks of our 2 daughters as I struggled with my own parenting skills. . .)

But regardless of "beginner's jitters", the *encouragement* mode is a friendly arena. It is rather flexible in the area of errors and failure. . . Children, also, are the most forgiving of beings. Not born perfectionists they are often better at being "humane" than we are. . .

> *I have encountered more reality-based greatness in the hearts of eleven year old dreamers than ever there was in the hormonally abject antics of many 40+ year olds. - 83*

## The Mentoring Process

Regardless of haphazard background experiences, the most significant mentors of children are their parents. Whether we are the best we are or the best we aren't, we are what our children have as parents. And as long as we are the best we can be, I doubt that our "normal" does much serious damage. And anyway, childhood is a process not a state. The forward movement it undertakes is one of "growing away from" parents and "growing towards" the larger world - and, as children never do things easily, both of these at the same time. It is in the nature of all children to immerse themselves more and more into a larger context where their being can be tested and their skills honed. Because of this, parents, despite all best efforts, cannot fulfill every area of expertise or responsibility where a child's progress is concerned. Nor should they be expected to - or expect to.

The concept of formal schooling and the superlative idea of apprenticeship programs were created for this very reason. And this from the very beginning of time. Sadly though, both of these *encouragement tools* are suffering in our age of "progress = change" and neither seem to be fulfilling the roles they were set up to play.

In essence we have made it more and more difficult for children to integrate into the world of adults. And at the same time we have made it more and more difficult for significant adults to have a healthy impact on children and teens. Results? Feelings of frustration, rejection and anger on all sides. Ultimately, children want and need mentoring, reassurance and eventual integration and if it isn't available at home they seek it elsewhere. "Families" - groups and gangs - are more than welcoming in our disenfranchised world. And these "families" willingly act as surrogate mentors to the increasing numbers of more than eager-to-learn youngsters in their midst.

## Blame It On The Parents (Again!)

Once, as "cave-parents" and "migrant communities", we mentored naturally. But with societies becoming larger, more complex and sedentary, the concept of apprenticeship was introduced. The goal was to offer our children an expanded life experience and the skills they could depend on to not only survive but thrive. Becoming an adult, once meant learning from those who already were. It meant gradually becoming a part of something "worthy".

Today, the definition of apprenticeship - of becoming, sadly has been distorted to mean nothing more than - preparing to enter the workforce. What once, required a growing sense of reliability, independence and maturity has shifted. Our adult tone has shifted. We prefer keeping adolescents young, dependent and "unworthy" of "our" adult ranks - even though our looks, attitudes and behaviours, at times, are far more immature than theirs.

## Life Experienced, Life Shared

Once, pre-teens and adolescents not only knew what their parents did all day - they were more often than not part of it in the sense that they could look up to and learn from the significant adults in their lives. Through mentoring they were introduced to "adulthood" - in all of its varied facets - both strong and weak, good and bad. And through encouragement, most children learned to pick and choose what they required to pave their particular life path.

Mentoring is now outmoded - a part of the past. In its wake a deep chasm between adults and children has been dug - one in which "discovering oneself" and being one's own person (whatever that means) over-rides family dynamics, community involvement and individual creative energy. The new "us", created by such a mind-set, more and more revolves around co-dependency rather than growth and the spreading of wings. And despite the new and improved personas that we purportedly are. . . we still feel lost. We worry excessively, have nothing to hang onto and are anxious about everything. And because we are and we do, we inadvertently transmit this lead weight to our children who, in turn, can't understand why this is happening to them. And when both adults and children in an environment become one in their frustrations a collective "aloneness" of discouragement isn't far off.

Once, children tagged along as co-pilots in their father's truck or their mother's never-ending world of caring and nurturing. They discovered what the work-a-day world was by being allowed into factories and offices, laundry rooms and cold-storage lockers, studios, grocery stores, kitchens, bakeries and print shops. Children got to know how adults talk to each other, deal with each other. They learned about team work and individual creative effort, appreciation and complex decision making. They had the opportunity to look up, down and sideways - to ponder, to choose for themselves whether this part or that part of the adult world would be theirs - or not. They could analyse and measure the personalities they encountered and discover what was or was not acceptable in this adult world they aspired to. At times, children and adolescents were given "real" work to do, given opportunities to actually be "valuable" to the significant adults in their lives.

I am not talking about re-introducing child labour practices, here. I am talking about allowing children to see and feel and know what it's like to be an adult - that nebulous thing they are becoming - and yet, weirdly know nothing about. Today, we don't so much meet children's curiosities through real-life experiences as we offer them compensations through lowest common denominator replacements. Why? Well, in our estimation (or at least that of the insurance and specialist child-rearing milieus) life is just too dangerous to be "actually" experienced by children and teens.

And so we create a mish-mash of inconsequential activities such as the ubiquitous "bring your child to work" days. . . and virtual realities through software programs which define to our offspring what it is "really" (?) like to be us. That such superficial connections to adulthood are valid is no more true than texting is excellence in communication. Such cosmetic add-on exercises do not provide anything real - anything tangible that children can grasp onto. But then. . . kids today are more easily endured when they don't bother us - don't interfere with the hectic worlds we ourselves haven't figured out yet.

## Denying Entry

And so, as our disgruntled and discouraged children grow, we basically are telling them that they are annoying, troublesome and immature. We even seem to hug them "away from us" - from who we are - rather than stimulate their pride and wonder in the process of "growing along with" the adults in their lives. We do little if anything to welcome them into puberty - this second birth in the life process of every human being. Why is it that, in our "contemporary" cultures, reaching adolescence is not a wondrous mystery celebrated? Why, rather, does it cause so much fear and apprehension in the hearts of adults?

Today, children are less and less excited about learning, about growing up. And that is simply because no one encourages them to. No one welcomes them and their eagerness to "be a part of" - to "do" whatever it is that would allow them entry into a world of responsibility and caring. But then, "to do" they must know - and to know they must learn and to learn they must experience. To experience they must be encouraged to participate and to feel deeply that they can. They also need to know that what they have to offer is *welcomed and respected* by the ever expanding list of significant adults in their lives. But the systems we have set in place for them are not encouraging. Increasingly, learning processes which demand excellence and skill acquisition are being eliminated - considered of no value. . . too "hands-on", too "labor" oriented - not intellectual enough. And yet, when intellectual aspects get too difficult - well - let's make that easier too. . . less stressful anyway. . . And when children realize that it doesn't really matter if they try hard or if they even try at all, what does that say to them? How can they actually think we care when idiocies such as the following statement (made by a high-school counsellor in the 80s) are made on their behalf:

> *"School is not simply about learning skills. It has more to do with gaining life experience which, when translated into a meaningful mind set, enlightens the emerging personal goals marinating within all of our adolescent souls". . . . .*

My "mind set" still dozes off - goes into a trance, when I think of the content value of such esoteric claptrap. But then, I realize that it is through the collective ramblings of (pseudo)philosophers that today's lowered expectations are formulated. And so, because of such fantasies we cannot deny that what encourages our children to think and dream and "want" to become adult, is gradually being eliminated from our academic "mentoring" systems. Whether it be in the arts, sciences, literature, history or languages. Everything is being watered down - in order to make it all palatable and our children "passable". Too much of what we do is end-run success rather than process oriented. Whether anything is legitimate anymore is irrelevant. Nonetheless, what is relevant is that our children are failing even though they are passing. And no one seems to find that disturbing. . . No one seems to take into account that the easy-success programs we set up for our children are more in keeping with making us look good than they are geared to their needs.

# BEYOND DISCOURAGEMENT – CREATIVITY

> *When "times are tough" the first cuts in education, municipal, provincial and/or federal governments, are always made in the areas of culture; i.e. visual arts, music, dance, theatre. But when those same institutions need to attract money from sources which highlight the viability of a sector, the first people recruited for fund-raising are those in the "artistic milieu" - the very groups and individuals who are so often considered superfluous, costly and irrelevant. -* 99

But academics are not the only subjects being watered-down. The very activities which are the foundation of success in the academic milieu (i.e. the creative arts) are increasingly being eliminated from the learning process. At the best of times, many school activities in music, performing and the visual arts are secondary in nature - add-ons to academic subjects rather than creativity in its purest form. That music and the visual arts contribute greatly to every other learning aspect of a child's life is unquestionable. And yet, schools simply mirror the general public perception of the arts, not its true nature. When there's money in the kitty, all kinds of "artistic" things are introduced. But when economies are weak and the need for creativity is ironically at its highest, these very programs are the first to be eliminated.

Never mind that music, the visual arts and physical movement are essential for minds and bodies to develop to their fullest capacity. At a time when we should be teaching children how to be astute in problem solving and solution gathering, we dull their minds with boredom, false aspirations and false grades - if their efforts, or lack thereof, are graded at all.

If children are to be *encouraged*, schools must become more than babysitting factories geared to passing them and their bored countenances forward from year to year. Children must be perceived as more than bodies to be moved along until they finally get to a "higher learning" experience - where (sadly) they must be told that what they actually need in order to succeed is ten times more than they have to offer.

All in all, our contemporary quest to keep our children safe, free from the worries, anxieties, responsibilities, tribulations and excitement of the world is beginning to cost. Through over-protection and hovering we have actually created the opposite effect. Children don't feel safe and they don't feel free. They feel stifled and discouraged from being and doing anything.

What the actual price to be paid for the end of the 20$^{th}$ century and the beginning of the 21$^{st}$'s slack and over-protective attitude has yet to be tabulated. But the costs will be high.

## Schooling Discouraged

Because children are born excited about learning, it is ironic that schools are not places children run to with impatient anticipation. I am not so naïve to believe children ever did. . . But maybe that says something about the whole idea of schooling. But, hasn't it evolved? Isn't it much better than it ever was? In essence, school has not really evolved in the past century. It has gone from being a place of excessive discipline - where children always wanted to run a way to feel alive and be creative, to a place of over-protection from which children's minds and hearts simply run away because there is "nothing" there.

Eager learners need an environment which greets them, which says your curiosity is important and your passion rewarded. Children must be part of a world which says "your wondering, dreaming, trying, testing, failing - getting up again and re-trying anew are recognized and will be respected". If the world truly loves its children, those self same embodiments of creative energy

# BEYOND DISCOURAGEMENT – CREATIVITY

must feel deep down in their gut that they will be encouraged to achieve at the highest level of accomplishment of which they are capable - and that this effort and hard-earned achievement will be celebrated.

But today we cannot bear, or so it seems, that our children "might" trip, fall or fail. . . Is it because we fear for them? Or is it because we fear being perceived as failures when and if they do? If so, that self-centered feeling on our part is not only sad, it is devastating to every individual child and the whole of our societies. Occasional tripping and pratfalls are part of what leads a child to new learning, new insights and adventures. Going beyond the safe numbing-normal of virtual realities and the anxious norms of our over-protective present are a must if our children are to take on the challenges of our contemporary worlds. Schools should be places where the wonders and worries and technical skills required to deal with those worlds are presented - not avoided, dealt with, not denied.

We have too many no-failure, no-error and no child left behind programs *which lie to our children.* Teaching them that failure is bad and errors are for losers is tantamount to making them fear trying anything now and later in life. If our children are learning that they should avoid any type of struggle or pain by simply "being" rather than "doing" (and I think they are). . . I must repeat. . . I am afraid for their tomorrows. . . and ours.

> *Ironically, educators have come to realize that "all" children are special and have a right to special education. But, still so mesmerized by this extraordinary concept, no one seems to have considered implementing the discovery - 03*

Nonetheless, children seem to have the innate capacity to be patient and forgiving - despite the adult foibles and anxieties which surround and, at times, strangle them. Unlike adults, they are resilient. Children simply want the opportunity to "understand". They want to know what happened before - what's been tried and even failed so they can try and test and conjure up new ways of looking at and handling things. Children look up to those who still consider them worthy of being taught, worthy of the whole idea of trying and failing and trying again and progressing and learning. They are extremely appreciative of those who lovingly take the time to share and teach them "the ropes".

But does wanting our children to thrive mean that we parents, teachers and mentors must be thoroughly informed about everything?

I think not. Though children request performance excellence from those who teach them, they do not demand perfection - so let's all breathe deeply. . . exhale fully and relax. Children not only want to learn from us they want to learn with us. They want to know that we still enjoy learning. Having us calm and confident is what children desire most. They profit greatly from a relaxed parent, one who does not constantly feel inadequate or gets upset when they have difficulty following through on the latest jargon or parenting technique being thrown at them. Children instinctively know they are not perfect and they definitely know (through concrete experience) that neither are we. And children don't care if "we" don't get it right the first time. What they do need to know is that when we don't, we simply pick ourselves up and try again.

# BEYOND DISCOURAGEMENT – CREATIVITY

## Ah. . . The Good Ol' Days!

Not so long ago, it seems, parenting was learned by osmosis - through traditional value systems which "once" were considered sacrosanct, invaluable to a society's survival. Adults simply carried over what they learned from their parents and grand-parents and possibly a live-in uncle or aunt. Everyone shared in the daily activities related to family survival. Though generational adaptations did occur, the core of family life basically stayed the same. And, through such consistent structures, societies progressed and thrived.

With several generations living together in rather small (for us) quarters, the environment in those far off times was always an area of shared experiences - both positive and negative. And yet, few children suffered from the various "isms" and symptoms we impose upon them today. Children, then, were too busy being needed and wanted and free - their eccentricities accepted if not endured, their limitations and exceptional capacities taken into account. No child was the same as another and that was expected - even appreciated. That some children were more boisterous or calm than others was not considered a perplexing or frustrating state of affairs. And "difference" was not perceived as an "illness", as it so often is today.

> *Children have always been wondrously wondrous.*
> *They are at the same time:*
> *the person we think they are*
> *the person they think they are*
> *the person they truly are*
> *the person we want them to become and*
> *the person they want to be. - 69*

When emotional aches did occur, there always seemed to be someone "available" within the extended family - available to calm or reassure a child. When mother was busy, big sister, brother, aunt or gran'ma was available to soothe an ache, listen to a woe, critique artwork, read to or hand out hugs and warm milk. But generally, individual quirks were sublimated, arising more during "alone" times. As a rule, there was very little opportunity to focus on details which were not conducive to communal living. Everyone was busy assuring family survival. 5 year olds picked eggs, 9 year olds cleaned out stalls, pre-teens fed and bathed babies and lugged in firewood. Teenagers groomed and fed farm animals and helped with harvesting and storage of foodstuffs. Then, everyone had breakfast, grabbed their "tools" and went off to school or work. There was very little time for looking in the mirror and doting on a navel-gazing "self". The victimhood of "Me-ness" had not yet been invented or universally applied.

But, as this is no longer the case. . . being as life is a lot simpler and yet a lot more complex - attitudes, activities, responsibilities and privileges have changed. Today, basic survival needs of families are more easily met through steady, if not large, paychecks. There are grocery stores on every corner. Dishwashers and electronic home gadgets of every ilk make our lives easier. But are our lives really better? Are we less busy, more free, more enriched, more calm, more content?

Actually, our lives today are more hectic than that of a 19th century farmer who left the house before daybreak and finally returned to the dinner table long after dark. Today, after a hard day's work, we race home to be on time to take our children to their play-dates, lessons, courses and team sports. Today, we work hard so that our children will not have to - as if this is a good thing. . . And when they are through with their scheduled activities, we are still not through focussing on them since we have yet to fulfill our quota of "quality time" - that time when we continue

# BEYOND DISCOURAGEMENT – CREATIVITY

to ignore our needs as adults in order to assure our increasingly tense, self-absorbed and anxious children that we love them.

And so, because we choose to direct extreme amounts of energy and time pampering our children the very opposite of what we are trying to achieve occurs. When we make our children's lives soft, the very core of the collective that is the family and the very unity which once assured strong communities begin to suffer. And this occurs for the simple reason that when one segment of a collective receives more than its fair share of attention 2 things begin to happen:

1. That pampered segment, at first, revels in the excessive attention then it rebels since it finds itself no longer able to breathe, to create to thrive. And if its rebellion is for naught, depression eventually ensues.

2. Secondly, the excessive nurturing of one segment destroys the needs of the collective which eventually causes the destruction of a society from within.

In essence, our child-centered mentality is achieving the complete opposite of its goals.

> *As with many social engineering concepts, child-centeredness has always been an iffy proposition. In small doses it may have some redeeming value hidden within. But in larger expressions of its philosophical meanderings, dangers abound. Its greatest flaw is that it presupposes that the adults administrating this "ism" are "adult".*

> *Apart from too often being a sham slogan for every new child-oriented or educational fad, child-centeredness is more a decorative adjunct to a self-centered adult world than anything related to better child-rearing perspectives. Foisting (abandoning?) adult responsibilities (and privileges) onto children and teens, under the guise of respect and equality, is not adult. It is immaturity at its worst. Despite claims to the contrary, child-centeredness is fast becoming what we seem awfully fond of creating these days - a syndrome. . . a syndrome whose symptoms are a hovering over-protection, abandonment of adult responsibility and an increase in self-fixated anxieties. The most devastating in all of this is that we actually think the contemporary state of child-centered families to be healthy and progressive. - 01*

Actually, how we now deal with our children as individuals and how we communicate our feelings and sentiments, and how we allow them to communicate theirs, is one of the areas in which *encouragement* is either real or not in our contemporary family structures and societies. Whether we live now or in the past is irrelevant. What we do with what we have "in the here and now" is what is important. Coddling, over-protection and hovering don't work. And the proof that they don't is in the lack of creative production inherent in our discouraging child-centered environment.

## Getting It Right

That we care about our children is not in question. We love to see them achieve and accomplish. We love being proud of our offspring. But when all the challenge is taken away from their striving, under the guise of protecting them, how far are we willing to go in order to make them feel "really" good"?

When we compliment them do we communicate *encouragement* or discouragement? From the time our children are little, do our reactions convey that they are fantastic, wondrous and beyond-real - when they do any little something? Or do we direct our amazed attentions to their accomplishments - to what they do? Which is the better reaction? Does it matter?

Essentially, it does matter what we say and how we react to what our children do. Patting a child on the head - i.e. telling them "what a sweet, good, wonderful beautiful boy you are!" creates a very different feeling in a child than does admiring his achievement. Saying: "I am truly impressed! This is excellent work! " conveys something totally different than blanket praise. But is the difference communicated that important? Why would there be a preference in a child's mind for one or the other of these reactions? Actually. . . there is a world of difference between these 2 reactions - especially when one or the other comes from a significant adult in a child's life.

Since the beginning of time, children have had to deal with having their efforts and achievements accepted or rejected, encouraged or discouraged. And from the beginning of time, they seek recognition for their accomplishments. They need to know that their efforts and interests are valued and their accomplishments appreciated. But what children hope for the most is that what they do (and how well they do it) will open the door of the world they aspire to so greatly - that world of adulthood . There is nothing that a child wants more than to be seen as "a viable candidate" for this arena. But it is often in this very area that children first discover disappointment and discouragement... So, when are children actually encouraged and when do they feel discouraged? The answer to that relates to how "personal" the reaction is. For it is when things get "personal" that hurts occur and scars last.

## The Do-Be Phenomena

Even though young children associate themselves closely with what they do they also know when to separate themselves from their actions - when it hurts and when it is discouraging. Adults are less proficient in this arena.

If a child "does something wrong" the reaction is often: "It wasn't me!, I didn't do it!" Why do children run away so easily from situations in which they will be "nailed"? The answer to that is easy... They ARE being nailed! No one likes to have a finger pointed at them and no one appreciates being punished. And no one appreciates being punished because it is more often than not VERY "personal" - and THAT hurts.

A punishment situation is for all intents and purposes always meant to be personal. In the eyes of a judging adult, a perpetrator is *bad* for having done something wrong. Therefore that person should be punished. But in the eyes of the culprit, the concept of personal is intrinsically wrong because the accusation is more often than not *NOT* about the bad or good thing done but "what kind of person" the one who did the dastardly deed is...

## Fantasy's Reality

Now, children are well aware of the concept of "being" and that of "doing". Their ability to differentiate between the 2 (beyond the age of 7 to 9) is not in question. But their capacity to formulate proper behaviour patterns is not always as well developed as they would wish it were. And that can get in the way of things going well. . . Now, an average 7 to 9 year old "is", in his daily life, what he "does". . . If that 8 year old stretches his arms out and creates plane sounds his running about, swooping and diving and soaring, "makes him" that plane or, at other times, the incredible flying ace. Children do personalize everything as they immerse themselves into imaginary personifications. If a girl dreams of being (and acts like) a princess, she "is" the princess. "Being" and "doing" within the realm of dreams and imagination are the same thing to a child. And imagination at its best is a child's world.

*But*, in the realm of reality, it is amazing how children have the capacity to appreciate what is real and what is not - what is correct and what is not. Over the many years I have observed children's behaviour, I have noted that they are most capable in the area of reality discernment strategies. They define doing as doing and being as totally another thing in the real world. While in reality mode, children easily discern who they are from what they are doing. Nonetheless, it is irritatingly discouraging to children when, more often than not, adults are incapable of separating these 2 entities.

When children do something perceived as "bad" (by adults) those self same adults generally get annoyed. And as adults are more often than not incapable of separating "being" and "doing", children suffer the consequences of this adult handicap which focusses on the perpetrator more than it does on the 'bad" action. And that's when things get "personal".

## To Be Or Not To Be...

Effort, application and hard work are things related to what we do or don't do. They are not who we are. Children older than 7 to 9 know that. Accomplishments or failures can therefore be good or bad without a child losing their sense of self - since - and I repeat - children separate failure, error or accidents from "personality". But adults don't seem to get this concept. And because they don't, children from very early on are forced to accept that accidents and behaviours are never as bad as *they* themselves are considered to be. In essence - and I annoyingly repeat again - when bad things occur, the focus seems to always be on the child and not on the act itself.

What we adults fail to realise is that it is difficult for a child to countenance the teeter-totter emotions which accompany our comments - as they relate to child "doings". Adults more often than not play the "morals" card. And because we do, our morally based reactions are "personal". Rather than admonish or commend in such a way as to deal with the action or behaviour itself, we impose the bad or good "feeling" on the doer.

In the child realm, this is not valid. It's not playing "fair". The morals of children are more abstract. They are tied to an action done - not to the person. They expect adults to understand that what they have done may be perceived as bad - but hopefully their connection with the significant adult will not be altered through their lapse in judgement. But sadly, personalizing reactions has a tendency to do just that . . . It renders interpersonal connections "conditional" - in feelings if not in fact. And whether we adults like it or not, children are "feeling" oriented. They know when the love they get is "conditional".

In essence, whether comments directed at children are negative or positive is irrelevant. As adults associate the child with the deed, that child finds itself in an emotionally precarious position.

# BEYOND DISCOURAGEMENT – CREATIVITY

With adults, everything seems personal - and therefore anxiety-provoking. Why is this? Well. . . the devil is in the details and that's where we often get lost. . . A case in point is that adults often say that a child "has done something wrong" and yet. . . when it comes to assessing and sorting our the situation the only thing wrong inevitably ends up being "the child" - not the "something". The same thing happens when a child is complimented rather than the deed recognized.

## The Gooey Approach. . .

At first children feel good, feel loved and cherished when they are complimented for having achieved something. Being treated wonderfully is always cause for a giddy reaction. That's a given. But gradually, children come to realize that adults do not talk about the accomplishment so much as they judge the doer in their complimenting. And this is when things begin to "feel" wrong - i.e. personal.

When a significant adult is pleased, children often find themselves being defined as "good" rather than having their actions deemed good. This causes warning signals to go off in the child's brain. Being as adults seem incapable of differentiating between the "being-doing" link in imagination and the "being-doing" separation in reality. . . the whole situation gets royally mixed up in the minds of a child and tensions begin to build. .

> *"If I do not achieve well. . . will I be perceived as being "not good? When I have done well am I then good? If I err, if I have an accident, if I make a mistake or do badly, am I then bad?"* It's all logical isn't it?

Now, complimenting a person is always personal. Its expression affects self-worth. It speaks of "the person's present value" rather than the positive aspects of an achievement or accomplishment. It infers that if they do less than their true abilities, they will (naturally) be less valued. And as time passes, and the analytical skills of a child improve, another seriously important "personal" emphasis comes into play: *how others see us is more important than how we see ourselves*. Personal comments, therefore, cause insecurity whether they are positive or negative in nature. Now, that is something to ponder...

Saying to children that they are wonderful because they have painted a beautiful picture is nothing more than a "left-handed compliment". It implies that *as they have done what is expected of them -* they are considered good. But it also implies that if they, at one point, produce a less good drawing, don't dance, sing, cooperate or play as well (i.e. they do not do as others expect them to) they may be perceived as "less than" they were prior to that action. And if this is so, children get the "feeling" that they will or may lose the previous recognition, affection and appreciation from significant adults that they once enjoyed. Logical? To a child it is, and to a child that is a scary thing.

Naturally, this is not a true perception of reality - but then a child is a child, not an adult. A child does not necessarily interpret attitude in an academic, linear or literal fashion. A child "feels" attitude. And because it does, it becomes anxious when those attitudinal variables produce incomprehensible "maybes".

Praising a child who constructs a flyable kite is not the same as saying the kite is superb - the job well done. And that is why the former is easily misconstrued as an incomprehensible (discouraging) "maybe" and the latter a "real" encouragement.

## The Unconditional Factor

But am I saying that plain, unadulterated, overt expressions of love should never be made to a child? No! Absolutely not! What I am saying is that timing and focus are important. Telling a child we love and cherish them and find them to be the best child in the whole universe is goose-bumps WONDERFUL for them to hear. Now, they know deep down that these are excessively exaggerated statements. They are not fools. Such "play compliments" are like a game - like their fun fantasies and imaginings - and OH HOW WONDERFUL it is to hear and feel such loving words from parents. Children need to know, for no other reason in the world than that they "exist", that they are loved. Such spontaneous and effusive significant adult expressions should be unabashed and repeated as often as both a child needs to hear them and a parent needs to express them.

BUT. . . those affirmations should be made when no other element in the child's life is at play. Expressions of affection must be *unconditional*. As such, they should never be attached to or depend on a child doing something well or not. Displays of affection should be spontaneous and separate from anything else. They should stand on their own as warm and heady feelings both for the child and for the adult.

Also, from very early on, children like to be in charge of whatever they do. Their actions feed their identities and fuel their exuberant need for more "doing" as they learn to increase the quality and sophistication of their "doing" repertoire. To children, the more challenging life is, the more wondrous they perceive it to be. Children simply get a kick out of achieving. Simplifying things is an adult-who-has-lost- the-pleasure-of-doing concept.

In essence, children are the consummate example of "doers". They are action oriented. Unlike some adults, they do not thrive on being "something for nothing". For example, in the adult world, many of us seem to need "titles" to feel good about ourselves. What we do seems never enough to meet our "need" to be recognized. We like titles because they are about who we are or perceive ourselves to "be"rather than what we do. In actual fact titles have nothing to do with "doing" anything at all. Titles are personal. They relate to our sense of self as it is defined by others. Take for example the title: "artist". In the world of healthy children, to be called so is unimportant unless pleasing others is more important than achieving. What is important to children with a healthy ego is doing; i.e. painting, drawing or sculpting. And for that you don't need to be "wearing" the title artist. And that is why for the most part real artists have the souls of a child rather than that of an adult.

## Power To The Creative People!

With time, children grow to enjoy the power that is available to them as it relates to trying and achieving - or not. They like to test what is or is not available to them. And because they do, choice is perceived as power. Even if they enjoy their work being recognized, it doesn't mean that a free child will maintain that "expected" standard forever. Sometimes a child wishes to know how far they can go - or not. What does it feel like when work - or no work - doesn't get accolades? Is everything still OK? When a child is comfortable in their skin, not afraid or not submissive, testing what choice is all about is not only possible and positive - it is invigorating.

It is when a child controls how and when and why they are "productive" that their ego or need to feel loved is not threatened. But when the status of their ego is in the hands of significant adults - anxieties often occur. In essence, the increasing capacity to choose is the power which aids in maintaining emotional stability and eventual mature decision taking. It is also choice which permits an individual to maintain a quality of life worthy of their aspirations. And when that is possible, "doing" something well becomes a matter of doing it for yourself rather than the expectations or demands of others. For it is only when a child depends on someone else's estimation of their value that he or she fails to take on the power and control over their own life - thus failing to grow into a strong and emotionally healthy adult.

This brings us back to the main point of our specific discussion: to focus on accomplishment and not the child. For what actually needs recognition is not the moral status or standing of an individual but rather their efforts - things which relate to determination and concentration - not the person as moral individual. To encourage is to objectively review and recognize achievement without rendering a "personal" judgement. An individual must always retain the power of "feeling and being good" as *theirs*. And *that*, for all intents and purposes, eliminates the superficial need for "self-love" - or, as it is more commonly defined today, self-esteem.

## Loving Me So Much

Today, the idea of "self-esteem" is "in". It is said to be at the root of emotional and mental health. To that I can only say: Hogwash! The intense contemporary emphasis on self-esteem is based on individuals having lost control over their own lives and destinies. Self-esteem, as contemporary mantra, has more to do with marketing than it does with human well-being. And as an appropriated commercial property, it is a rather dangerous element in that its focus is more hype than encouragement. It is more associated with navel-gazing and entitlement than striving and achievement.

Today's repeated use of the term self-esteem is nothing more than a plasticized, externally pliable image of ourselves.

The self-esteem movement entices young and old to look at their reflection, as in a mirror - to see themselves as beautiful - just because they are. The activity is self-centered - and yet, after we have encouraged a child to focus on that "beauty", what's next?. . . If this is all that is required of a child - if this is as far as a child goes. . . when will someone offer that individual a hand to grow beyond themselves and out towards the rest of the world? Or is the realization that one is beautiful all that one needs? If keeping a child enamored with their own uniqueness is considered "healthy" how can the environment which encourages this be healthy? That we are collectively embracing and even encouraging narcissism as a child-rearing tool is rather a frightening idea.

Children should not be taught to define themselves through a superficial acknowledgment of their goodness, their self-proclaimed beauty or their mirror-based value. When times get difficult, as they inevitably do, a self-esteem mantra can't but fade - and when it does - it will always fail to live up to its own hype. When children discover that all they have to do is "nothing" - that all that is required of them is to "be", they soon learn that nothing provides them with the only offering possible in such situations: emptiness.

## Doing Is As Doing Does

Children cannot be connected to nothing - especially, they cannot have nothing to do. They are born being what they are: "doers". As such, they value their capacity to test and achieve and try over and over. Being recognized for their accomplishments allows them this necessary luxury - this encouragement to go on. As they grow, they begin to see that what they do not only is important to themselves but it also is valued by others. This connection between an encouraged child and the "world beyond" is crucial to a mind which thrives on creative energy. Becoming an engaged individual and a dedicated citizen within a collective depends on such encouragement playing a part in a child's everyday life.

Now, there is a definite difference between the quality of achievement in children (when they know adults are looking for good work) and that which is produced when they are perceived as "being good" for doing it. The former elicits feelings of excitement at the prospect of once again engaging in a new challenge. The latter creates anxiety as the results may or may not afford them the expected status.

When an encouraged child undertakes a project under its own steam and that project fails, everything is recoverable. Research, analysis and trying over and over are possible because no ego has been destroyed in the execution or reaction process. BUT for these retrials to be of any value - to be of service to the active child - the so-called "self-esteem" (actually: self-worth) components of that child's make-up must be intact - not as a feeling of entitlement but rather as a self-assurance of ability.

In essence, much of what is described above relies on the reactions of an adult. Is that reaction a personal judgement or a perception of an effort or an achievement's value? Every child needs to be clear on this issue. And every adult should be clear on the expressions related to it.

## What's The Goal?

Again. . . and it can never be asked too often. . . Do our reactions imply that a child is not good due to failure? Are children as expendable as the missed achievement? Or do our comments recognize that a failed effort is nothing more than a trial - i.e. a failed attempt which, as a learning experience, provides us with information opening the doors to an eventual successful try?

As significant adults, our goal should be to render children strong, to make them independent and capable of formulating new ideas and solution-solving techniques. If our need is to strangle this reach for freedom and independence (this gradual "moving away from us") whose needs are we really trying to satisfy? Contemporary parenting, as defined by a collection of pocket book gurus over the past century, has given us a series of bad habits which need to be broken. Some of the worst are the following:

- Hovering (the action of limiting a child's existence to our controlled space - as defined by our fears and anxieties).

- Looking at our children as fragile innocents renders them disabled not enabled.

- Buying them everything they want teaches them that nothing has value and that they are entitled to whatever they demand.

- As individual human beings, children and adults are "equal". But treating children as equals in reference to status within a collective is a lie. Children are dependent on their parents and mentors for guidance and reassurance until they are capable of being on their own. Schools and homes are not democratic institutions. And the sooner children and parents realise that, the saner family life will become.

- Filling their every waking hour with activities, outings and events teaches children to remain dependent - incapable of managing and organizing their own time and interests and unable to endure in-between times.

# BEYOND DISCOURAGEMENT – CREATIVITY

- Pushing a child so hard that "we" are upset when they don't achieve to the level we expect them to is nothing more than an admission that their failure is a reflection on our parenting abilities.

- Seeing every "difference" in our child's personality as a potential symptom, syndrome or disease. Labelling children and subjecting them to the myriad drug programs established to subdue enthusiasm and creativity has become not only an international crisis but more so an international disgrace. What we do to our children in the name of care is becoming frightening.

- Praising our children rather than encouraging their efforts simply discourages them.

In essence, our obsessions have to go. Really they do. Though we are more child-centered than ever before in the history of man, is it possible we have lost our way? Is it possible that child-centeredness has nothing to do with children? Is our focus nothing more than a focus on "our focus"? And is this causing a diminution of our children's talents - and, even more sadly, our children's uniqueness and ability to grown into healthy adults?

As we begin to recognize that these habits have more manipulative than actual value - and at their worst are seriously dangerous, we need to instill in our children (and in our personal perceptions) the appreciation for an earned self-worth - not an entitled "self-esteem".

But to offer our children such a gift, we must first look to our own motives and to what makes us "tick". Are we proud of our own achievements - in whatever field these may be? Do we want more than we are willing to do? If we were in the realm of the arts, could we find pride and enjoyment in being dancers, painters, sculptors, videographers, poets or pianists? Or would our needs revolve around recognitions received through status and position and titles such as "star" or "artist"? Is being something more important than the doing of what we do? These are some of the questions we must ask ourselves. For, how can we teach our children to be proud of their accomplishments if how we look at our lives and the concept of "doing" as av negative or as never good enough?

## Tools Of The Trade

And so, questions must be asked. . . Things in general must be wondered about - goals and focusses re-evaluated. But there has to be a catch. . . Right? This idea of *encouragement, to be embraced,* has to cost something. . . Everything else does. Every new way of handling our modern children ALWAYS has a dollar sign attached to it. First, let's discuss the contemporary assumption stated above. . . that to stimulate creativity, to be a good parent and to make your child a successful human being you need "the money" to get "the right" specialized, up-to-date tools, books and other "educational" paraphernalia.

The simple response to that type of thinking is the following: The financial costs of *encouragement* are minimal if not, in fact, non-existent. But, if we wish a more definitive - a more professional reaction in regards to the need for serious financial expenditures in the exercise of *encouragement*. . . here it is: Hogwash! Raising a creative child is not riddled with hidden costs. People with absolutely no funds have been doing it for centuries.

# BEYOND DISCOURAGEMENT – CREATIVITY

(And now. . . 2 really long sentences - even for me!) . . .

1   Encouragement does not demand that a fortune be spent on so-called educational toys, games, art materials, music, karate, football, tennis, hockey, macrame lessons, Stradivarius violins, ultra sophisticated, colour-coordinated outfits or anything else remotely related to specific and specialized products or "name brands".

2   The most encouraging thing I can say at this point is that no child on the face of the earth will ever have an advantage over other children simply because our pocket books cannot handle the "absolute requirements" of a specifically laid-out and professionally designed commercial process whereby a child's ability to succeed is purportedly guaranteed.

*(Complex sentence structures, maybe.) But re-read them and see how simple these thoughts are.*

The value of so-called educational tools is highly over-rated - especially when compared to the impact of a huge refrigerator sized cardboard box on a 5 year old's mind. Such an item holds more creative potential than at least 75 professionally designed and tested toys - (batteries and specialists included). *Encouragement* is an attitude NOT a bank account killer. Encouraging creativity does not mean spending your life savings on specialized camps, extensive field trips, day or overnight excursions, one-on-one specialists, encyclopedic coffee-table pop-up-picture- books or even the latest in computer technology. Encouragement *especially* does not depend on sending your child to the "right" (read: expensive) daycare, pre-kindergarten, kindergarten, elementary, high school, college or university. But it does depend on we parents being reassured that the primary focus and philosophies of the schools our children attend are based on encouragement and not on lesser considerations such as status and the seemingly ever-constant recruitment of funds.

Actually, money often gets in the way of encouraging creativity and its eventual expression. Lots of money is more a smoke screen than a requirement. The overuse of money, as a key element in the area of creativity, dulls the senses and falsely links creative outlet to name-brand fallacies and questionable in-house commercial "research" - which always tends to prove the educational value of yet another $199. product. Parents beware!

> *If truth be told, The greatest financial outlay related to creative potential should be in the areas of providing our children with healthy food and adequate sleep - 10*

An encouraged child is a creative child - whether that child lives in a backwater area of China, India, Canada or the United States or is the most well off child with the advantages of the best toys and schools in those same countries. Children need to know that it is not who they are, or where they come from, or how much their parents are worth which counts but rather what they do with what they have - and what they achieve despite the so-called odds against them. Children need to realise that those who "make it" in life do so not because they are rich or poor but because they take the ordinary things they have and do something extraordinary with them.

> *Success is not doing better than another but rather striving to do better than the best you you did yesterday- 09*

## Computers

All I say may sound wonderful in theory. But what about computers? What about the technical "essentials" required to maximize encouragement of creativity? There has to be some "'thing" which makes creativity possible?

Here we go again. . .

Advertising compels us to purchase the latest in anything and everything. And most of what it sells is related to creating and satisfying a "want" and not a "need". Day-in and day-out we are being pushed to get the new and improved. And today, there is definite pressure to get the latest and best in computer paraphernalia, (to enhance our children's creative impulses, naturally!). But let's get real. Computers are wonderful. There is no denying that. They are fun and they are also serious tools for many professions and trades. There is no denying that either. But necessary to creativity? *Necessary* for children to learn, to be creative? A necessity for the achievement of success and world competitiveness in elementary and even high school? Though many would argue pro-computer, their arguments would be based on doubtful suppositions. Granted, computers are wonderful learning tools, but necessary? Computers cannot stimulate creative impulses - especially in children who seem to have lost theirs. Computers are not the answer for children who from the very beginning have received few if any tools in the areas of mathematics, reading, writing, composing, understanding and general problem solving.

On a recent trip to Ireland, my wife and I were treated by friends to a visit to Sherkin Island, off the coast of West Cork. Not far from the ferry dock and just passed the ruins of the Friary, there it was!!! a mystical something which no one expects to find in this day and age. Giddy with excitement, I asked a stupid question. (I know, I know. . . There is no such thing as a stupid question.) But I asked the adult reading near the stone fence if this small building is what I thought it was - a one-roomed school house. The teacher laughed and said: yes.

10 children attend Sherkin Island school - and yes, it is a one room school house - and yes, children learn and seem to be quite sociable and content in their small academic environment. Some of them speak with us - intrigued that we are intrigued.

The school has no gym, swimming pool or fancy football field other than the freshly mowed lawn leading to the water's edge. Recess means that the children are all physically active and "in charge" of their own activities. They organize their games and the attendant (and ever-changing) rules. On that green strip of land overlooking a bay I listen to voices of completely happy children. The school itself is as equipped as required - but no more than needed. Some computerization is available but not "high" on the "necessary" list - especially since much of the atmosphere and learning process in this tiny enclave seems to depend on children being as independent and adventurous and as creative as possible. How more positive can an environment be than that?

What a delight such a discovery is in this year of 2010! A model for the rest of the world? It is not trying to be. It meets the present needs of its elementary pupils from the island (and an additional student from the mainland) with the expectation that when the students leave they will have what it takes to face "higher learning" and the world. In essence, it is not trying to "look like the best". It simply is the best for the people involved. And if their knowledge were tested on an equal footing with "more contemporary schools", I would wager the children would achieve with distinction when compared to students of the vast factory schools of our large urban settings. Good schools cannot be measured by size nor the amount and intensive use of technical gadgetry. But by the look of most schools you'd think a competition was on.

At an elementary level, computers are nothing more than shiny new add-ons with very little true value in the academic lives of children. To many of us, technical equipment is easily available and because it is, it plays a much greater role in our increasingly sedentary lives than it does our creative efforts. Helpful, though not necessary in the school setting, home computers are more often than not filled with "what I want rather than what I need". Their purpose is to keep kids busy and out of our hair. And no amount of elementary school time is required to make expert "computer users" of our children. They do that despite us and would achieve well despite no computers at all being in their classrooms.

At times, computers also serve the purpose of taking ourselves out of ourselves - of being reality avoidance tools rather than priceless learning apparatus. Many children have a computer in their "private bedrooms". It is therefore not surprising that the social network clicking, internet surfing and games (increasingly violent in nature) have it easy with our offspring. After an hour or so, getting them to join the family for dinner or other activity becomes difficult, unless that is, they simply are allowed to switch to their cell phones or gaming tools - where they can continue "socializing" during dinner - just not with us.

As for the closed door computer environment of our children's bedrooms, the question is not whether that apparatus is a creative tool but rather "where" and "with whom" our children are spending their time on line? Unsupervised computer use is more often than not simply virtual "baby-sitting"and "pseudo-communication", controlled by children and teens with no input from their parents.

But isn't that particular state of affairs ironic when in the same breath so many adults criticize computers and the internet as being dangerous? But please don't get me wrong. Computers in and of themselves are not "bad things". The key word, here, is "things". And in a bizarre science fiction way, these things are rather clearly "the future" surreptitiously unfolding itself before us - the robot luring and leading the human child away from us before our very eyes. And this is happening not because computers are bad but because we allow them to be emperor-like - controlling and domineering - and, ever so much more important to our children than we are...

All of this notwithstanding, computers are now an essential tool in all facets of *adult* business and professional life - essential to contemporary living and international communication. Does this mean that I am back-tracking and admitting that they are essential school tools? No. Children at an elementary level do not "need" computers. They need to learn how to read and write and count - independent of crutches and achieving based on their own mental and emotional steam. And in line with that, they probably would do better if school budgets focussed more on soccer, basketballs, pianos, books and painting easels as well as more time for running around during longer recess periods. That being said, computers meet our needs more efficiently when they are more closely monitored and their use structured to serve rather than amuse. When amuse is the focus, they meet wants not needs. At an entertainment level that's fine. But when fun is equated with making things easy... Computers begin to deflate our capacities to think and feel.

But being the mysterious tools that they are - when computers do good they do very well. One of my favourite television ads extolls the virtues of a basic yet sophisticated computer use. The particular ad in question is for Oreo Cookies... (Ahem - no promo is intended and no fee was paid...). In this product presentation, a boy "in his part of the world and in one time zone" is talking via videocam with his dad who is in "another part of the world and time zone". Their "moment" - each in his own other world - shows them "sharing" an Oreo cookie moment. Both thoroughly enjoy each others company (and antics) despite the distances between them. Rarely have I seen a more pertinent ad in how to make superb use of a computer. (Naturally, because the ad is beautifully produced, it does not take away from the main focus. . . those luscious Oreos. . . Ha!)

Silliness aside, the closeness and warmth displayed in the ad are palpable. The creative way of using a computer to hold close a loved one is wonderfully rendered. The ad shows the child to be happy. He does not need his father to be at his side - just available. Such independence in a child that age is wondrous (though ever more rare today).

Travelling parents often suffer the distances they encounter in their work - but this ad shows that both parents and children can survive anything - if they are creative in how they maintain connections and in how they perceive a situation like "distance" to be. As displayed by the ad, the problem of distance in a healthy environment is an adventure, not a cement wall as our neurotic contemporary attitudes often make it. A tearful distance becomes a positive connection and a difficult reality a manageable occurrence.

Computers, in other words, are not the problem. How we make use of them often is. In essence, they are useful and convenient, but necessary to encouragement and to an evolving creativity in children? Give me a break! Their availability, their prevalence in our societies has made them toys rather than tools. Their attractive "play features" lure us away from life more than they entice us to learn and grow and profit from the freedom they purportedly offer. So, once again, it is not the tool but our perception and use of it which fails us.

BERNARD POULIN

## The Packrat Environment

But, despite our modern era's exciting tool chest, electronics are not at the top of the heap in the area of creativity management. Children, whether from pre-computer times or from this age of high tech connections, resemble each other more than they are different. Simplicity in their lives remains an important catalyst for *encouragement* and creative potential. From the age of two years, children get more mileage and stimulation from paper, (lots of it), pencils, crayons, finger paints, glue, watercolors, plasticene and clay, than *any* commercially promoted toys. Wooden blocks, in various shapes and sizes, rhythm toys, illustrated books, music, puppets, cardboard boxes and discarded adult clothing are imagination stirring items which most wonderfully fill countless hours of creative time. Most of these "tools" are either inexpensive or free - and all of them stimulate the one area of a child's being that is least paid attention to in this oh so technical age: *the imagination.*

But as computers may not be the creativity tool of first choice, neither are the obsessively accumulated toys, and games piled high and crammed into each and every corner of our family homes. These hills of half-used, abused, broken and quickly forgotten items do nothing more than make the life of everyone, including the child, miserable.

Children do not need hundreds of useless, expensive, so-called education-oriented, adult-dictated, television and parent-magazine promoted toys. Their overall collective worth is extremely limited if not seriously exaggerated.

Sometimes, it seems, families go on outings simply to get away from the one place where each should feel comfortable, safe and content - the home. The toy "litter" in many houses has become so pervasive no one can enjoy the "family" space because no family (let alone adult) space is left. So where's the creativity in that? Where is the warmth, growth and happiness in that? Better to have a flowing imagination dreaming of doing something exciting than being forced to play with a toy which always seems to force its own limited agenda on our children.

## The Quality Time Factor

Once again, the byword (and not the "buy" word) to all of us parents is: Relax! Our children can keep busy without all of the "new and improved" garbage which passes itself off as stimulating and "educational".

Sitting cross-legged and "properly" in the living room, sharing an imaginary cup of ooooooolong tea with a talkative 3 year old (accompanied by 3 favourite teddy bears and a rag doll - one ear missing) is nothing less than encouraging. Such an encounter offers more encouragement to a child's creative potential than any commercially promoted, specialist-suggested item of dubious distinction. Anything that purports to do more for your child than its own superior imagination is not only being hypocritical. Such a claim is nothing more than an outright LIE!

And so... With the question of excessive amounts of required money having been slapped aside we come to another sticking point in the area of encouragement and creative activity...time.

Yes, raising a creative child does mean you have to spend some time (even if that is extremely little) with your child's insatiable curiosity and desire to discover all there is to know. Kids have this thing about them... Along with wanting to know, they like to be seen AND heard... They like to communicate and, more often than not, that comes in the vein of Why? What? Where? When? How? And Who? It's a wonder most children don't end up being journalists! And, as from the very beginning, parents are the only recognized genius-like creatures (!) in a child's early years. And, as such - they're the ones nailed with the questions which constantly need answers. Children associate "big" with smart. . . And so, at least for a little while, we can con them (and ourselves) into believing that this assignation of genius is actually true. . .

OK. . . Back to serious stuff. Re: the question of time. . . Let's be reasonable. Most parents DO NOT have the wherewithal to spend all the so-called quality-time our children purportedly need in order to be emotionally healthy. If truth be told. . . children aren't that crazy about spending hours on end with their parents - or, as we euphemistically call ourselves today: our children's "buds"!

Since the beginning of time (and certainly before the illusions of the child-centered age) parents have been busy doing what parents do. . . They work at work, then work at home - cleaning, washing, cooking, fixing, renovating, moving and snoring in a chair, exhausted after only 2 pages of a bed-time story. . .

And do you know what? The world keeps on revolving. And is the problem re: quality time the fact that mothers "today" work outside the home? Give me a break! Our grand and great-grand-mothers worked long and hard at their farms and in factories. They chopped wood, gardened to feed us and shingled roofs, while their husbands were in the fields or other factories - and together, and with no time for quality time, they managed the impossible - i.e. to keep roofs over our heads and their children relatively healthy, happy and sane. Parents in the "good ol days" had no more time for "quality time" than contemporary mothers do. So, let's stop the anti-working mother rants right there. Let's give credit where credit is due! And, let's stop all the imposition of guilt by those who ( being oh so saintly) drive their kids crazy with all of their imposed "quality time" activities. Sheesh! Rendering mothers guilty for simply doing what mothers have been doing for centuries is a farce at best and sinful at worst.

# BEYOND DISCOURAGEMENT – CREATIVITY

Whether an adult works outside or inside the home is irrelevant. Parents do not have as much time to devote to children as so-called authorities purport they should. And so what! The question is irrelevant. Children not only need that time to play with their real friends, they *prefer* playing with friends their age or even alone. Friends aren't always on about rules and proper ways of doing things. They aren't always controlling the directions things should go or how high a swing should swing or how fast you have to run before you fall "on purpose". . . In essence, the whole quality time, play-date concept has become much more a parent thing than it is a psychologically sound mental health priority. At first, the idea was a good one. It just got side-tracked into such a formality (by those who would have us all cloned) that it has lost all credibility.

Now, I can't dictate what other families do or choose to do. I can only look at my own family's evolution and discuss its quirks and realisations. Suffice to say, neither my wife nor I have ever punished our kids with "quality time". Being just too busy was our best excuse. So, we figured that the only way we could be "good" parents was to consider any and all opportunities spent with our children important. That meant getting used to the idea that "our family's " satisfactory quality time could be anything from:

- 1 second winks at a distance of 30 feet,
- 10 minute sit-down discussions,
- 2 1/2 hour TV movies (all curled up on the corner couch with requisite popcorn),
- complaint sessions where the kids would have their say and, in the end, we would "be the boss",
- 1/2 hour story-reading times, or
- the blowing of snotty noses.

Both my wife and I "work outside the home", as in: we both have a job. The difference is that I do my work "in the house". She goes out to work. Marie has always traveled extensively due to her various jobs. On the other hand, my being a painter (arteest, that is) means that working from the attic or basement is not a problem. I love it. (I am typing this in my pjs! - I know. . . too much information!) Actually, this fact allowed our 2 girls (as children) to not come home from school to an empty house. It means that they spent a lot of child and adolescent years with good ol' dad (me!). After school they would do their homework sprawled on the art studio floor. (And, 'gasp!' I never once used a germ spray on that paint infested, paper cuttings, canvas, chalk and dust strewed floor!!!)

I would paint or draw. They would write, read, add or subtract. And we'd talk, and talk and talk. I doubt their teachers would have appreciated the lively and lengthy discussions about anything and everything un-academic. The dubious quality of crazy antics - generally perpetrated by (you guessed it) would also have been considered "inappropriate" I am sure. The only thing I didn't do was help them with their work. . .

I wouldn't know the difference between a trigonometry equation and an iguana gullet if my life depended on it! Whenever there was a dramatic melt-down based on "I CAN'T do this!" My supportive answer always involved something like: "Sorry. . . Neither can I."

I can't say that the girls lost out due to my being "unable" to help. (Actually, they probably got better marks because I didn't.) I think fathers have a special "different" role to play in the lives of their children. A definite sign that the parenting job wasn't too badly done is if your kids still speak to you after they are grown-ups.

Keeping that in mind, I wrote the following (tongue-in-cheek) many years ago. But I still believe it to be true.

## BEYOND DISCOURAGEMENT – CREATIVITY

*A father's role is to teach his children that there is more to life than eating all their vegetables, combing their hair, sitting up straight, keeping their room "neat" and washing their hands before dinner. A father's role is also more complex than being the family brute or demander of straight "A"s. A father should teach his children about challenges and how to face them, no matter how difficult or surreal they are. . . A father is one who can get his children, even at a very young age, to deal with problematic or boring times and turn them into extraordinary ones.*

*But most of the time, being a successful father is not complicated. Though mature thought and responsibility are required, quality fathering mainly revolves around helping a child create his own excitement - making an ordinary day extraordinary. Being a father involves instilling in a child the concept of silliness - the precursor to healthy belly laughs and giggle-fits. A good father teaches his children to never take themselves too seriously. He teaches them to deliberately and secretly wear mis-matched socks or pants on backwards . . . . just for the fun of it. . . . for a whole day. . . without being caught by your mother, a teacher, friends at school or even by the local crossing guard. . . And a father of this high caliber is also one who teaches his children that when such a feat is achieved. . . this is what constitutes one horrendously successful day! A father who succeeds in giving his child such a taste for the absurd, is one who also displays awe at how long bubblegum can actually stay glued to the under-seat of grandma's favourite chair. . . how wonderful red and gold and purple sunsets are and how fascinating cats whiskers can be when they flutter. . . He teaches his child that (swear to god and hope to die) when you lie at the foot of a tree with your eyes closed you can't tell the difference between how a drop of rain feels on the end of your nose or how bird poo feels when it does the same. . . Now such a man, such a father can rightfully say he has gifted his child with maturity, feelings of self-worth and sanity when he has bestowed upon his loved offspring such wise-man gifts of wonder and silliness - essentials in the survival of all humans in a cockamamie world. . . - 95*

Now, back to the more serious stuff. . . The daily in studio meeting of "the wild ones" lasted well into their teens. And it all began out of necessity and parental preference. Suffice to say, after all those years of ordinary "quality homework time" we 3 are still the most talkative, giggly and extremely silly threesome you will ever find. How my wife and their mother Marie endured her "3 kids" all these years is beyond me!

All of this to say. . . time spent encouraging a child is often more valuable when peeling potatoes than when it is a planned experience or scheduled event. When children, wearing a chef's hat, kneel on a kitchen chair "mooshing" crackers, using a potato masher with both hands, no more beautiful sight or quality time event could ever be planned or formalized. Such time is neither "made-up" nor forced. It is natural and warm and "feels" good. Actually, "mooshing" crackers can be for no other good reason than to give a child something to do while, "together" in the kitchen, you seriously analyze all the problems of the world. One wonderful kitchen memory for me involves meal preparation time with our eldest daughter Elaine. When she was 6 or so, she and I would pull out all of the leftovers from the refrigerator in order to create exotic "new" recipes. Sometimes we'd roast the concoctions or fry, or boil, or steam them. (Naturally, we'd only do this when Marie was away on a business trip. . . ) The time taken was meal preparation time, so no more "quality time" than usual was required. Elaine is now 40 and we laughingly remember those weird and wonderful recipes to this day. Though we seriously considered writing a "left-over" cook-book together (!!!) we wisely gave up on that idea. . .

Being as I am singing the praises of my parenting techniques (Do you actually think I would point out my numerous errors and all out dumb moves???) I also selfishly claim to be responsible for steering Elaine into gourmet cooking. And as long as I am taking *all* of the credit. . . she also ended up running her own most successful gourmet food gift basket business where all of her own jam and jelly creations were highlighted. Did I mention that in 2003 she won the best small company award in our capital city's region?

(Note: Taking credit for everything accomplished by a child is the natural prerogative of a parent. . . Ha!)

As long as I'm on a roll. . . I also claim to be the encourager of Valérie (our youngest daughter) regarding her forays into the unknown - beginning at the ripe old age of 2. Naturally, I would never attribute this early independence to her own head-strong attitude or my lack of supervision. . .

Actually, Valerie would disappear and I wouldn't know where to find her!

Usually she was at the neighbours - helping to weed his garden while discussing the national debt. . . Otherwise, she was on the swings in the backyard of our "across-the-street" neighbour - where she wasn't supposed to be.

Obviously, the above information is loaded with self-centered humour but it doesn't take away from the fact that my hair began going gray early. . . (Losing a kid for even a minute is very scary!) But for the rest, my only real claim to fame is that I was "there". My wife Marie, on the other hand, has always played a major role in the encouragement of both our girls. As far as Valerie is concerned, she and her mother are like two wirelessly linked Blackberries. . . . As if through osmosis, Valerie has assimilated her mother's political, administrative and business instincts and acumen. She has become a successful professional woman who at a very early age took on and succeeded in the most demanding world of politics. (And this is a totally unbiased observation, I assure you!) And now that I am finally being truthful, Marie over and above her fantastic professional achievements is the "real" chef in our home... (She does the actual cooking. I'm good for one thing: grocery shopping.) Marie's influence on Elaine's gourmet style and success was much more tangible than mine ever was. If truth be told, Marie was and is a most creative and incredible role model. She is the prime impetus behind our eldest daughter Elaine's strengths and giving nature. Elaine's instincts and deep spirituality, which gives her the soul of an angel, come from her mother I can guarantee you that!

What I am saying through this family voyage (apart from the heavy dose of bragging) is that if a couple should have screwed up, it would have been us... Most "new" parents have no idea what they are doing and that is actually the best trait parenting partners can have. When you think you know it all you really don't. Your kids will make sure of that...

Our greatest advantage was that we were born in a time when it was OK to think outside the box. Based on traditional family and community values we simply, expanded and added to our repertoire of parenting skills (or lack thereof) as needed to meet the requirements of "our" environment - never mind the neighbours. Despite the numerous "specialist" books touting the virtues of every "new and improved right way to do things", we just did what we did without thinking or worrying about what we were getting into. Probably, we were too busy to think about making a mess of it all... And probably things moved too fast for the problems to catch up to us.

All this to say that none of us out in the real world has time for formalized "quality time". Trying to be a perfect parent is not only a lost cause, it is senseless. None of us are or could ever be perfect. "Good" times are those which make us smile - whether they are silly or serene. More often than not, true connections with our children involve nothing more than a loving wink, a moment to smile, a millisecond hug. And those are the makings of wondrous memories and the greatest of old-age reminiscences.

Quality time is an attitude - more of a psychic, spiritual or emotional presence than a concerted physical one. And it is what a child feels and not the hours and dollars spent which make a difference in their budding attitudes, adolescent maturities and ongoing creative potential.

## Down The Rabbit Hole

The most important thing is to get our children to realize that WE are thrilled with their curiosity and their wanting to know. Our children need to feel that we are excited about what they say, see, question, wonder about or even hate. The essence of an encouraging presence is "interest", coupled with a neutrality of criticism - a greater awareness of critiquing rather than the running down of a person, thing or idea. If anything, our children are ecstatic when we are awed by what fascinates them - no matter what our own personal interests are. What they appreciate in the end is discovering what makes us curious, what our tastes are and what special thing takes us "away from it all". And in the end, they will take the interests of others into account because we took time to consider theirs.

If anything, animated conversations with parents do take children "away from it all" to areas of their and our brains that we would never have expected. Being open to any and all discussions creates and rekindles creative fires in children. It eggs them on to even more discoveries and wonders. And as bizarre as it might seem to us, when children are curious about a topic, they may not even know where it will take them or why. And this "not knowing" doesn't frighten them in the least. "Mindless inventive adventures" and discovery are exciting to healthy children. They need to fall deeply into whatever it is they are dealing with. And when we share such excitements with them they are thrilled.

Children love to float freely. They enjoy every minute of a "getting lost in it all" feeling. At first, following them down into Alice's rabbit hole may not be a comfortable experience. But that reticence is natural - we're adults. We lost trust in our imaginations a long time ago. And because of this we are more comfortable leading our children down paved roads then following them down a dark forested path. Actually, we're more inclined to clear any and all debris, pitfalls and unknowns in our child's way. . .

But sometimes. . . the natural expert is the child and we are the apprentice. Sometimes it's best to let go, to let them lead. It can be scary but often it is exhilarating.

# The Child-Parent

Throughout this "child-oriented" mayhem of our times, we shouldn't kid ourselves. . . our children want to know what WE think - at least after they've had their say. And, children are incredibly generous. . . They don't care if we don't know anything about a specific topic. What they do care about is that when we don't. . . it doesn't embarrass or upset us. They need to know that "failing" to know is not a bad thing but rather a stimulus to curiosity and for a learning to take place through a shared research experience. All in all a positive attitude, in regards to wanting our child to be creative, is worth more than hours of what we so euphemistically call "quality time". . .

## BEYOND DISCOURAGEMENT – CREATIVITY

> *I want to share in my child's life as a valuable parent should. But, kids prefer their parents to be parents - not chums. . . It is a serious mistake to not know the difference. - 84*

## Availability And Possibility

But in my quest to offer encouragement in the area of creativity, am I not forgetting that a rich environment filled with exciting venues is more appropriate than one in which the creativity enhancing cupboard is bare? In other words if we don't live in a full service city isn't the potential creativity of our child toast? Are children who live in the country, or far from major centres, at a disadvantage? Nay-sayers be forewarned, there are no areas on this planet which can be considered voids or vacuums.

The possibility of creativity flowering in the hearts and minds of children is not limited to those who live in larger cities and towns. For the many in remote areas, creativity and growth thrive not because of availability and possibilities but despite their purported absence. Small country towns offer as many possibilities for exploring as do big cities. The context and discoveries are simply different. There are no fewer eureka moments to be made and discussions to be had in a town or small city than there are in New York, Paris, Beijing or Vancouver.

Libraries, community centres, local theatres, school halls, church basements, community gardens, creek beds, ponds, lakes and rivers, airports, malls, hay fields, barns and a myriad other natural and exotic settings have much to offer. "*Il s'agit d'y être ouvert!*". This French phrase says it all: "You just have to be open to what is". Small factories, farms, and sole-owner businesses are extraordinary sources of information which can stimulate creative development - (even with pre-school children).

Becoming aware of what is available is a parent's second step in the encouragement of creativity. The first is to recognize that the environment, from which your child embarks on a voyage of discovery, is the foundation upon which creativity will blossom. All in all, it is often surprising to note what and how much is actually "there" in our very own back yard. We simply have to recognize from the start that there is something there.

Eventually though, children will want to do more than "look and take in". They will want to participate, not just observe what they have discovered. Children want to be a part of whatever they have discovered through you. This decision should be encouraged. Before and after outings, discussions with children are incredible eye-openers. And during these times, both parents and children discover the each other in a new light - one which revolves around a mutual excitement and discovery.

## Time Out!

Now after all of this mamby-pamby writing about how wondrous and extraordinary and totally super-duper our children are. . . maybe it is time to take on a subject which deals with how our kids can REALLY be. . . Let's talk about time outs. . .

Traditionally, the contemporary term "time-out" has been used as a disciplinary tool - an ethereal "place" children are sent to when they are not behaving, as in: "You are getting a time out from regular play or other activity because your behaviour is unacceptable. (Read: "You're driving me nuts!"). Time outs are a sit-out time away from other children or stimulations - or so this control technique is supposed to be. It's a calm down tool for a child so that the parent can un-frazzle in peace and quiet.

# BEYOND DISCOURAGEMENT – CREATIVITY

However, this technique can be altered to mean something else - something which, once discovered, could almost eliminate the need for the "negative" type of time-out.

*(Did you really think I was going to actually write about how bad our kids can be!?)*

Time outs, at their best, can be specified times for relationship building and communication. I prefer this type of time-out as it implies that both the child and the adult are "taking time out of their normal day" in order to meet both of their closeness needs. In such a scenario, where time out does not mean "you have been bad", a child learns that "resting a mind, heart and soul" once in awhile during the day is a good thing.

Depending on the age of a child, the length (rather than the duration) of a time out can be 5 to 30 minutes. During this scheduled period, both adult and child can share an activity, such as play acting, listening to a made-up song and dance routine, or simply chatting and enjoying a glass of milk and 1 or 2 of those "chocolate circle thingys with white stuff in the middle. . ." The key to such get-togethers is to make them the least bit formal. Not everything parents do with their children should be an "event". Maybe, get-togethers should be just that: getting together just because we want to talk and cuddle and ask questions or just sit and read or simply be together. . . .

Time-outs of the positive kind should never be a chore - but something that both individuals look forward to. Such time-outs can even be skipped some days or multiplied whenever required. Good time-outs are not absolutist-based. They're free and are wonderful because those involved "choose" them.

Time-outs give adults a chance to switch gears - get away from everyday "adult" demands as well as ease up on accumulated stress. The child also profits by calming down excess energy and/or by getting an adult's "undivided" attention for a specified amount of time. Though not a formal activity, such sessions should not be disturbed by phone, cell or texting calls, (incoming or outgoing) - or by visitors, unless they accept to take part in the time out. This is crucial as children most often lose out whenever another "all-important adult" or another child (older or younger) enters the picture - monopolizing "their" time.

If a child is confident that he/she will have their "special time" each day or every other day, or whenever both parties would "like" to have one, they are less likely to demand excessive amounts of attention during those periods of the day when adults are busy with "adult" things and they are doing their "child" things. A child should also feel that this time out activity allows for"upsets" to be brought to the table for discussion. They should learn early that sharing is not limited only to fun good or happy things but sad and angry things too.

Time outs can happen as many times a day or every other day as required; depending on the child's age and personality needs. As an example: one is often useful in the mid-morning, one in the mid-afternoon and one in the evening, when quiet reading, story-telling, chatting or just plain hugging time calms the child before sleep.

The results of planned time outs are often the following:

- a calmer child
- a more curious and adaptable child
- a warmer relationship between parent and child
- a more patient child who respects other peoples' busy times
- close times

But what if this sharing technique has never been used in our home? How do we go about getting our child to accept our "new and improved" communication offer? I would suggest making an

"I have an offer you just can't refuse" offer. (You can bet your bottom dollar that such tactics are *not* beneath me!)

Example: Introducing a healthy time out to a child can be as simple as announcing: "I only have one can of soda and (time to whisper in their ear) I know we shouldn't be having one because drinking soda is only for special times. . . But. . . (Here you should wink) would you like to share it with me?"

Now, if your child is incapable of submitting to that heavy-handed manipulation, cum bribery, cum con-artistry, I think that kid is taking life WAY too seriously. . .

## I 'Vant' To Be Alone!

Now, positive time-outs are not the be all and end all. But, through them, both parties come to realise that there are also positive benefits to the equal and opposite alone or independent times. Accepting that a child is capable of and free to comfortably do things on their own is *encouragement*. Children need to be alone - to "be with themselves" - to do things which mesmerize or simply interest them. And if we respect these times, they too, in turn, will accept that adults need time away from them. Children do comprehend balance - time together and time apart. And, through recognized times alone, children also learn another important concept: the different makeup of lonely and solitary times.

In essence, "I am free to do as I please without interference times" become precious. To a child, they become "my" time. And this opens the door to their creative explorations. It is a time where they can dance to music they prefer, draw or paint, read or play with plasticine, dig for worms or take an old clock apart - create monsters and characters and animals in clay, cardboard or sticks - straight from their imagination. So, positive time-outs not only mean better and closer communication, they also mean better and warmer "separations" which respect each individual adult and child need.

## Artwork Display = Recognition

In the first 5 or 6 years of childhood, doing things on our own, often means (if we are lucky) drawing and painting "freestyle" rather than in colouring books. Such free expression is a wondrous activity since a child's visions, perceptions, understandings and curiosities can often be more easily expressed through artwork than through words. In the toddler to young child years, recognizing their abilities and interests in the areas of self-expression is of prime importance. Children love to test art equipment, paints and plasticine - to see what these tools "do". They love to "formulate visual thoughts" but they also enjoy having those thoughts appreciated by others. This validates their efforts and ideas.

But sadly, when it comes to the visual arts, children are often limited to colouring within the lines of a prescribed book. This limits their exuberance and teaches them to follow "rules" as established by an adult prescribed "need to be neat" formula. Naturally, all of these controls negate the very idea of creativity and limit self-expression to "acceptable" parameters. If any funds must be expended in the area of creative self-expression they should be allocated to 3 foot (91.5 cm) wide rolls of brown wrapping or "newspaper". They last forever, cost little and are immediately available whenever the artistic muse strikes.

But whatever the medium or the tools, children's artwork needs a forum - a prominent display space in the home. Their work represents how they feel and how they interpret the world around them. And if they are ever to consider themselves worthy individuals, those perceptions need to be acknowledged. Reactions of: "It doesn't exactly go with the curtains. . ." has only one result - a fussy child in a really neat (read: sterile) environment. Lack of recognition not only reduces artistic output, it eventually eliminates it. But that does not mean that scribbling on the walls with Crayolas or paint is allowed. - *not even* with washable colours. (Living in a collective does require curbs on excessive exuberance. Freedom does not mean licence, even for little tykes.)

Also, exhibiting artwork does not mean a child's self expression must take over the house. The usual space is often the best. For example, there is always the refrigerator door. Or, if a more formal (or larger) display space is preferred, a reusable metal or wood frame can be purchased to hang artworks in a living area other than the kitchen. (Hint: photography and craft shops and department stores are great places to find various sized inexpensive frames whose "backsides" are easily removed and reused.) When this route is taken, every now and then you can house a different drawing or painting produced by the young Picasso.

But be careful. Not everything children do is a masterpiece . . . nor should it be treated as such. If all children have to do is scribble a few effortless lines or shapes to get squeals of delight from significant adults. . . what's the use of working at it? In such a situation, crap = excellence = crap. When there is no difference between working hard and sloughing off. . . A child learns quickly that working hard is a waste of time - because there is no real recognition - just excessive gushing.

What a child needs to know is that adults recognize honest effort and special work which tests their imagination. But most importantly (and actually, this is the crux of the matter) a child needs to hear the work being praised and not that they are good for having produced it.

## Meeting the Needs of Picasso

So. . . Children like to express themselves. . . But isn't allowing self expression in the very young dangerous - as in - "look at this holy mess!!!!"? Certainly it is - unless we are proactive. While it is important to recognize children's creative efforts, the enthusiasm they display in that expression can be problematic. Channelling exuberance is often a matter of "where" this creativity takes place. Every home, therefore, needs an area where creative juices can flow with total abandon. Otherwise...

This can be a bedroom, garage, family room, playroom, basement workshop, a table in a quiet corner, a kitchen window seat or even a back yard shed. Where depends much more on how much mess a parent can endure than how much space a child needs. The primary reasoning is that children must feel free to be "messy" in at least one area of the house. They must be able to concentrate on what they are doing and not worry about nagging rules regarding tidiness and "ruining the dining-room floor". Creativity can be and often is messy. (That's a given.) But without a designated space, children soon begin to feel like (1) boarders in the home rather than members of a family or (2) their mess can take over the house because no one says anything to the contrary - and so, they continue being the rightful tyrants that they have been given permission to be.

# BEYOND DISCOURAGEMENT – CREATIVITY

Nonetheless, if every area of a home is a "no mess zone", children soon submit to the feeling that who they are and what they have to say are unwelcome. If cleaning up gets more attention than creative effort, children eventually tire of trying to be their "creative" self. And when that is the case, being annoying starts to look pretty good after awhile. . . It demands much less effort and certainly compensates when self expression is in need of. . . well. . . self expression. So how do we go about accommodating the early years of artistic genius?

As we are basically talking about keeping a house livable it behooves us to seriously consider limiting the "damage" a young John Singer Sargent or Andy Warhol can bestow upon a home's interior. From the time they are very young, children love colour and paints. They enjoy manipulating them and expressing themselves with their hands and fingers and brushes and crayons. Parents, on the other hand, cringe at the thought of "one child plus one set of bright paints"!!!

If this is a problem, (short of covering a whole room in oilcloth), the bathroom is a godsend. As a studio, it is inexpensive, efficient and limits the "chaos" to a few square meters of bathtub or shower space. But, how do you go about creating such a studio? First, plan out the idea based on the following questions:

*What is the goal of such an art studio?*

- Provide a nag-free space for self expression which limits the expected "colourful" chaos

*What are the equipment requirements?*

- 1 tub, (non-skid surface a must)
- Paints - water soluble - (color choices belong to the "arteest")
- brushes, paper, masking tape

- 1 home-made table-tray, (see sketch)
- Finally: 1 naked, (nude?), happy child, any age

*What is the procedure?*

- Tape one or several sheets of paper to tiles or walls of bathtub enclosure
- Place tray in position, (see illustration)
- Fill butter, margarine, yogurt or cottage cheese bins with non-toxic children's water-based paints
- Add brushes
- Add child to bathtub studio
- Close shower doors or curtains (optional)
- Let the self expression begin

*What are the clean-up procedures?*

- When activity is over. (Naturally there is colour all over the place! What did you expect?)
- (Save complaints til later)... Begin by admiring artwork - reminding yourself that it was NOT created in the living-room.
- Do not hug child at this point... (unless you wish to become part of the artwork!)
- Remove table-tray
- Leave child in tub. My seriously adult comments at this point usually run in the way of: "OK... Time to get all this blue, green, yellow and red blood off you!" - I know... Gory and immature... But 3 year olds find it funny.)

# BEYOND DISCOURAGEMENT – CREATIVITY

- Run bathwater/shower. (Close curtain or door!) This will wash away excess color from walls, tub AND... artistic genius

- Your job is to clean the tray and brushes. (Not a bad trade-off...)

*Additional advantage?*

- There wont be any arguments about whether it's time for a bath or not!

In essence, encouraging creativity - is not rocket science.

*The making of a studio tray:*

1   Measure the width of the outer-edges of your tub enclosure

2   Cut and sand 1 plywood or plastic sheet: approximately 32"x12"x1/2" (Get it cut to size by your local lumber emporium staff)

3   Jigsaw 4 to 6 holes into which yogurt or margarine bins or cups can sit. Allow for wider cup lip

4   Insert cups into jig-sawed holes. And voilà!

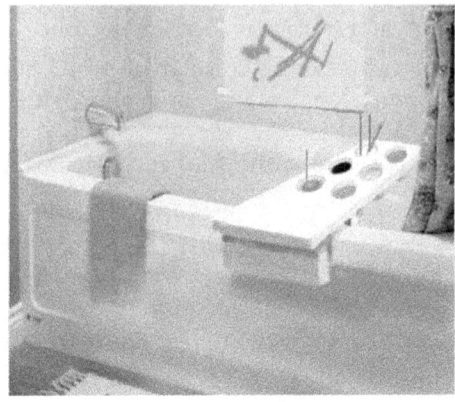

All in all, the studio-bath idea is not the result of genius thinking. It is simply a common sense plan in a family setting. And the main results can't be any better: everyone's life is a lot more "calm" and congenial and the artist is happy.

## Individual Interests

As discussed previously, encouraged children like alone times - times when they discover themselves as one of those wondrous and "capable" beings of the world. When I was a child, my greatest weekly pleasure was to be told by my mother on Saturday mornings, (after chores of course) "Here's your lunch - and don't you dare be late for supper!".

Now, I am well aware that in this day and age, allowing a child the freedom to roam, explore and discover on their own constitutes neglect, rejection or some other form of child abuse. I just thank my lucky stars I was a child then and not now. In our family, my mother standing at the door handing out lunches was tantamount to being given a "get out of jail free card"! It said we were trusted to go off and "do whatever" it was we wanted to do AS LONG AS we followed "the one cardinal rule": be home in time for supper.

## BEYOND DISCOURAGEMENT – CREATIVITY

Tantamount to holding fledglings out over an abyss - and bidding them fly, this meant I could wander off to parts unknown, to fields and creeks and railway trestles, to roads never crossed and always fascinating tree-tops and dreams never dreamed. My favourite was always the creek near the "Decalcomania" company. There were always leftovers from the factory lying about and the sewage was always so colourful. . .

In essence, wherever alone times take place, is where the imagination and the "possibility" batteries are charged and discharged and re-charged again.

Allowing children freedom to experiment, test, explore and question is crucial. It validates the personal directions they choose to undertake. Letting them examine the "makings", the construction, the elements, the details of objects, tools, crafted items, cloths, buttons or abstract ideas gives free rein to curiosity which encourages even more exploration and analysis skills to be assimilated. The very existence of things and places unknown opens the door wider to children better understanding what makes them and the world "tick".

Solitary pursuits also permit children to concentrate on a hobby or activity which demands total commitment of their mind and senses. Activities such as collecting stamps, buttons, coins, rocks, shells, bugs, bottle caps, hockey and baseball, soccer or basketball cards not only help define individual interests, they help define who we are now and will be in the future.

Even team sports profit from the participation of children with healthy creative egos - children with a sense of self. Without them, team sports would be populated by nothing more than inflated or deflated egos desperately trying to show how much better than the others they are, instead of those who are there to participate and share in the team's spirit and goals. Whether through painting, sculpting, carving, electronics, piano, mathematics, science, violin, flute, dance or theater, individual interests not only substantiate the passions within us, they give our life a rhythm and disciplined foundation upon which our adult lives can be built.

## But There's Nothing To Do!!!

Amazingly, when creative energies are part and parcel of who children are - they are rarely bored. Not only are they capable of keeping themselves busy, but their minds are programmed to reach out and discover even more. Healthy children have a capacity to fill voids with enthusiasm blended with a calm yet full determination that is rather incredible to observe. Now, this is not to say that "normal" boredom doesn't occur. When illness or listlessness happen (due to tiredness or having been made to wait MUCH TOO LONG for adults to get their act together) children do fall prey to boredom. Even as adults, we have those moments. But in the healthier portions of our lives, boredom doesn't have much of a hold when our psyches are programmed to forge ahead based on other alternative personal interests.

Children who are bored when they are without a planned activity are discouraged children - incapable of formulating "void-filler" plans. To them, life is a programmed environment, a vacuum, an empty space which must be "other-driven" rather than personally driven. Being alone for them is a matter of loneliness not solitude.

> *Boredom is either a door through which one passes to reach the complete darkness and paralysis of despair or through which one discovers the tingling attraction and sensual pleasure of a creative response to the nothing that boredom emits.*

> *It is the glass half empty or half full; the thick darkness of night or a rich and deep backdrop to the stars. . . Creativity is the ability to make something of nothing. - 02*

## Failure

Naturally, in the pursuit and exploration of things children will encounter "failure". Success at every turn is not what life is about. Failure is a part of daring, of being fully alive. But a child encouraged is one who takes all of that in stride. And because such a child does, failure does not feel like "failure". An encouraged child knows that not achieving or "winning" or succeeding is not personal. When encouragement is part of a child's life, it is not the child who fails but rather the outcome of the exploration or activity which does.

Failure, when encountered by an encouraged child, is an occurrence which actually stimulates the mind and determination rather than discourages it. It forces a child into a "questioning and curiosity mode".

> *Why did that happen? What did I miss? What can I do to change the outcome? Where can I get more information? Who can I ask? What else can I do to change the results?*

Encouragement is evident when children come to see "un-success" as a challenge, a search for an elusive solution rather than a stain on their ego. Now, while trying to do things on their own may work some times, children soon come to realise that some problems require help - collaboration rather than a solo foray into the unknown. And when that occurs, their personal arsenal of weapons against ignorance is strengthened. This is when they discover that requiring assistance does not diminish their powers.

It doubles them. When failure is not personal, the problem remains the focus rather than the self, And because this is so, children, through team work, become more receptive to the creativity of others.

## Going It Alone?

Though children enjoy doing things on their own (they feel powerful when they do) this is not always possible, or at times, even recommended. Not even adults do everything on their own. Parents who want the best for their children certainly know that. And though they remain key (the mainstay figures to an encouraging environment) teachers and mentors must also play a role in defining the parameters of a world of *encouragement* to a child.

As stated previously, children are programmed to grow and a major part of that growth is slated to be "away from" their parents and their families. As children expand the borders of their child and adolescent worlds they grow more and more towards friends but most especially to the "core self" which allows them to integrate more fully into the world at large. In essence, the ultimate direction for all human beings is towards a contented solitude within a collective environment - a place of community in which it is possible to maintain a unique outlook and creative presence.

To achieve a more solid footing for a child in this "impossible to stop" quest, it behooves parents to allow as much "other" input as is possible. As children grow they must know how others think - others who are not their parents or family members. As their quest is to gradually establish themselves in the world, children must integrate the thoughts and feelings of other significant adults and peers in their life. It can only be detrimental to a child's progress to limit their potential - by restricting other influences and visions.

## BEYOND DISCOURAGEMENT – CREATIVITY

The concept of mentoring is age old. It has been with us since the beginning of time. The young have always been influenced by those who come before them. Mentoring allows children to expand their perceptions and horizons. Through mentoring, children learn about becoming a man, becoming a woman, becoming citizens, participants - what it is to be a member of a society. It is within a child's ever-expanding world that the learning of expectations, of selfish and selfless thinking and action, of individual thought and collective reasoning takes place. The more children grow away from their core family, the more they must feel that they are getting closer to being welcomed into an adult community - a society in which they can play a part - their own unique part.

But, adolescents today are not comfortable. . . They feel that nothing seems to have been planned for their admission to the world of adults. In fact they feel so unwelcome that the sentiment is one of being pushed away. Part of the problem lies in the "stranger" phenomenon - where the concept of "strange" in the word stranger is emphasized. This perception is compounded by an era in which emotional roots are deeply sunk into a quagmire of anxiety and mistrust regarding anyone who is not related or anything which is not "usual" to the family core. And with this ingrained mentality, the very persons who daily try to meet the needs of our children, (i.e. teachers) are also pushed aside as detrimental to the progress of our entitled children. And as the insularity of families grows the capacity of our children to integrate fully and creatively into a larger world fades.

> *What contemporary fear has done to us all, as individuals and as nations, is almost impossible to fathom - 05*

## Shades of Patricia Cayo Sexton

Boys especially lose out in this most crucial aspect of their lives. Despite the modernization of academic systems, schools whether elementary or secondary, still fail to meet the requirements of boys. And where the academic milieu goes so do guidance and mentoring. From social expectations to reading skills - schools are more and more oriented to a sedentary teaching and learning style. Over and above an unbelievable negation of the arts and "physical movement" as essentials to skill and creativity acquisition, school systems perennially fail to take male (active) learning needs into account.

In the past fifty years, learning environments have not so much evolved as they have simply added new features to the status quo - a Model-T Ford to which a 2010 air bag has been attached. Despite budget increases and intense scrutiny over the past century, our educational systems have not come up with the promised "results" - i.e. more informed, trained, independent thinking and competent graduates capable of taking on any and all challenges the world has to throw at them. And because they have not, academic offerings and expectations are quietly being dumbed down. The whole concept of achievement is being revamped. Failure is being eliminated from any and all lexicons, from kindergarten to university. Basically, children no longer need to achieve in order to succeed. Increasingly, excellence is scorned as "élitist" and *undemocratic* while lowest common denominator expectations and choices become an acceptable norm.

Such environments inevitably bring on feelings of discouragement in both students and teachers. And when "not learning and not achieving" happens, mentoring as a source of encouragement is quasi impossible to implement. Are we saying to our children: "We're not too sure how important we consider your present and future lives to be."?

## BEYOND DISCOURAGEMENT – CREATIVITY

It certainly seems so.

> *It is not that we are a more stupid people but rather that in fear of being discriminatory we have come to perceive and celebrate ignorance and banal achievement as near genius. - 01*

## He Shoots, He Scores!

But even in areas where mentoring has had a strong traditional foothold, things aren't what they seem. Organized sports have long played a major role in defining who and what an individual can be within a collective and collaborative environment. Yet on their own, organized sports cannot fulfill a mentoring mandate. Winning has become too large a component in the overall team sport picture for true mentoring to take place. And, as losing relates to more teams and therefore more individuals than does winning, the present picture is exactly what it implies - only a few can achieve where the rest must simply accept that they are not winners - especially if their time on the bench exceeds the time spent actually participating in the sport.

The above comments are presented only in reference to the problematic context in which we presently live - not as a rejection of the best of what is organized sport. My days as a basketball, handball and hockey player were never stellar. I was rarely part of a winning team. But the context was different. Being perceived a winner or a loser "in the good ol' days" did not carry the heavy connotation it does today. And unless some of us were so highly competitive that losing (in our own mind) made us feel like victims, we pretty well went off to the pool or tennis tables, marble patches or card games (!) to try our luck in another arena.

In essence, there are few venues other than sports where boys feel they can shine. And this makes the loss of superior mentoring, once universally available in these activities that much more sad. Add to this that, today, many contemporary families are either blended or single-parent in nature and the problems are compounded. Despite best efforts on the part of parents, boys once again fair badly. Their need to identify with and understand their own "maleness" is not being adequately addressed and, actually, in our western culture it has rarely been.

Being such an animal... (i.e. a male - which often times simply means a boy grown tall) I can attest to a world where boys are often perceived as disturbed when in actual fact they are nothing more than "disturbing". In regards to this comment, I encountered a neighbour some years back who, after seeing a gaggle of "lively ones" go by, loudly proclaimed that at 5 years old boys are too rambunctious for their own good, at 8 they are incredibly obnoxious, at 10 impossible, and at 13, downright dangerous...

After that fascinating pronouncement, I was happy to see her re-enter her abode. What with being only 25 at the time, I was sorely afraid of how she would depict my errant age bracket.

It is difficult for boys in that, from the start, they are often considered a species anomaly - their behaviours and mannerisms delinquent rather than simply different from more acceptable (read: compliant) girl attitudes. Boys simply don't fit the "good children" mould. Even their physical and neurological development leaves a lot to be desired as far as our learning systems are concerned... Their small muscle co-ordination is slow to get established and their capacity to read and write slower than the expectation standards set in stone by school officials.

But there is one thing about boys which is universal. They are born hero worshipers. From a very young age, they seek to emulate significant adults with gusto. And, for better or for worse, when they can't find a hero close to home they look elsewhere.

## BEYOND DISCOURAGEMENT – CREATIVITY

When boys succeed, they are extremely proud. But they are even more so when they have someone to look up to who is proud with them. Encouragement of all children is extremely important. But, if an encouragement scale can be applied I would say that the encouragement of girls is most important - for boys, it is vital. Often times, the person they wish the most was at their side is not. Boys need their father, an uncle, a grand-father. And when that is not possible - a Big Brother. To state that the need for encouragement is great cannot be over-emphasized.

Does this feeling of being alone upset boys? Yes, but not "obviously". Despite our purported modern perceptions of maleness, we still aren't comfortable seeing a boy cry or express sadness - even when things get rough. And being alone without someone to look up to (where boys are concerned) constitutes rough.

As prime candidates for mentoring, boys need a clear message from all directions about what is or is not excellent in the process of growing up. They need adult guidance and very little of it is available to them because we don't often see, understand or even consider their specific needs to be crucial.

In writing these latest paragraphs on mentoring, I looked back on my life. Amid the encouragers and discouragers I met along the way, there were a few who are worth mentioning. I recommend this exercise to everyone who cares about children and adolescents. If we've had good and/or bad mentors, it's worth the review. Getting more acquainted with "if and how" these people influenced our lives gives us a better idea of where we come from and how we got to be who we are - AND. . . How we can be the best we can be in the mentoring of children.

Actually, discovering that we haven't had any, or very few mentors, is also an important discovery to be made.

In the completion of this exercise, I realise that I was quite lucky. My life has been filled with a balance of both uncaring and caring men and women. From the time I was very young, I encountered all manner of personalities - some positive, some negative, but all influential. Some espoused mentoring naturally - encouraging me as best they knew how. Others seemed to pride themselves in discouraging me at every turn, But I learned from both.

Generally, parents don't fall into the mentor category but I do consider mine my first. My mother taught me laughter and gave me an appreciation of both music and the visual arts. Today, all three of these "gifts" are very much part of my life. My father, despite never having had the opportunity to do what he would have loved to, was an excellent mentor. He taught me 3 things also: that I should always try to do better than my best (with whatever I had) because, as he put it: "That's all there is". He taught me that a painter may be an artist in his studio but beyond it ( holding a painting under his arm) that person is a businessman - either selling an idea or selling a commodity called a painting. Thirdly, he advised me that the myth of "the starving artist" could either be my fate or a choice. I could either accept or not this illusion of pseudo-masochistic grandeur or go beyond it and leave fakery at the doorstep. (He wasn't interested in his eldest son starving for a living - and he wasn't one to suffer fools gladly either.)

A cub scout of the 43$^{rd}$ Mowgli pack in Windsor Ontario, my mentors were mainly women - i.e. Akela, Baloo and the others who ran the cub pack meetings. As in most aspects of a child's early years, women are much more prevalent as mentors than men. They seem to better understand and fit into the mould of the communal concept of mentoring responsibility. For the most part, men still have difficulty grasping the idea that their very "maleness" offers that "something different" which both boys and girls need to know about in order to become fulfilled in "the becoming of who they are". Children need the influences of both sexes if they are to understand their own life progress.

## BEYOND DISCOURAGEMENT – CREATIVITY

How children react when they are mentored by women is not the same as when they are being encouraged by men. Though I learned much from Akela and her very patient female crew, I do admit that my intent at that time was more "to please" than to achieve. More often than not this is a boy's pattern. He strives to please the significant women in his life but wants *what he does and how he acts* to be recognized and approved of by the significant adult males in his life. But, regardless of my psychological "interpretationeering", thank you Mrs. MacDonald (Akela) for your encouragement, solid moral teachings and for the simple fact that you cared.

At 9, I loved my mathematics teacher. She was an older nun living in a convent near our home. Through an errand for my mother, I discovered the grand lady that my teacher was. Walking the length of the corridor to the Mother Superior's office, I came upon a crumpled and diminished Cinderella-like servant - on her hands and knees, scrubbing the tile floor. The wondrous figure stopped when I passed, raised her face and stared at the perplexed 9 year old that I was. She smiled warmly - and I, shyly back to her. That day I received a first lesson in grace and humility. (Regarding those. . . I am still very much a work in progress.)

At 10 and 1/2, I was enrolled in my first art class - learning to paint in oils. I was miserable. The teacher constantly corrected my work. She never explained what I was supposed to do. She never encouraged any of the students. After one grab too many at my paint brush, and one more correction accompanied by discouraging sounds, I had the first tantrum of my life. Immediately ousted from the class, I was brought before the gallery director, my equipment and wet panting in hand. (Shame on me!) After listening to the teacher's complaint about how horrible I had been to her, the director escorted her out the door. Following her departure, he spent some time in total silence, staring at my scribbles and strokes. Finally, he said "Go home and paint. One day you will be a painter." And so I did. . . and so I am, and I thank artist Kenneth Saltmarche, for that superior moment of encouragement. No boy interested in the arts could have asked for more. At 12, Reverend Father Rosaire Laflamme, o.m.i. became my spiritual advisor. He was an odd little priest at the boarding school I attended. He taught me that if the intentions of my heart were true, the rest of me was bound to follow. He introduced me to patience and to love the work I did. He believed in my artistic abilities (if not in my bad Latin declensions). And for his caring presence at just the right time in my life, I am eternally grateful.

At 14, the owner of Famous Furniture in my home town hired me to paint landscapes. *(Lord, they were horrible!)* He would insert them into frames from which he had extracted cheap reproductions. He sold my work as "real" sofa paintings for more money than he could have made from the reproductions. And so, he made a profit and I did too. We were in business. . . I learned about "production" and being respected as a man. I thank him for trusting me and for proving my father right. . .

At 15, Jack Kennedy (my high school English teacher) taught me to stand before a crowd and "roar" with conviction. Though shy, I came to love words and self-expression - and through him, reaching out and sharing. I remember him fondly every time I start a new book or begin a series of lectures or workshops.

At 16, I was repeatedly told by a clergyman at my local church that I was basically "lame" as a human being. He said that I would never amount to anything. I always wondered whether he was more disgusted with himself than with me. Nonetheless, I thank him for having pushed me to strive even harder - if only to prove him wrong.

It was also around that time that I chose to go off on my own. . . To leave home for good, to quit school and move to another city. (No. . . My parents were not charged with neglect and abandonment. . . And no one came running after me. . .) That decision meant I had to get a job, pay rent and feed myself. And so, like all others who decided to do such silly things at such an early age, I did. I was eventually hired as a stock clerk by Milton Shaffer of Shaffer's Mens' Wear In Ottawa Canada. But I wasn't there for more than a year and a half. Mr Shaffer fired me - telling me he didn't accept that I would be a stock clerk all of my life. He then "ordered" me (the very independent teenager-cum-professional man) to register at a school - any school. He added that I would no longer be welcome at the store until I could prove I had registered my participation in some academic institution or, I could come by if I needed clothes.

Though angry (in a typical teenage way) I did as I was told. . . eventually graduating from Ottawa University Bilingual Teacher's College. I enjoyed a successful career in education and subsequently started a career as an international portrait painter. And what of Milton Shaffer? Well. . . He is 94 years of age and still a much loved friend of our family. All in all, mentors are important. They define more clearly who we are and eventually become. The more a child is encouraged the stronger they are. They need this strength to fight off the discouragement that lurks in the dark corners of our sometimes bizarre environments. When mentored, when encouraged by parents and others, a child feels more and more invited, more and more welcomed into the world of adults by those she can look up to. And when children do feel welcomed and respected, the more determined and successful they are as adults.

Therefore, to those who generously mentor I raise a glass of admiration and love and appreciation. *Encouraging* the young to be the best they can be is the most noble way to live a life. And to all parents I say: Let your children be touched by the lives of others. They can only be enriched and strengthened by them - and, for that, your children will thank you.

## Summing Up

And so, we have looked at many ideas whose sole purpose it has been to stimulate yours. We have encountered creativity as a wondrous and necessary thing - whose primary support network is based on *encouragement*. This life enhancing element may be difficult to implement at first but the results are so incredible, even the most rigidly cold amongst us cannot help but admire them.

We have also examined the devastating effects of discouragement as, like a viral infection, it crushes spiritual breathing - the very lungs of growth and human flowering.

As adults, we have examined a specific point of reflection which stipulates that ours is a responsibility of *encouragement*. Ours is a quest: to bring children to realize that to be the best they can be they must do the best they can do. Because without the possibility of doing there is no "being" worth being. . .

## Le Partage
### (The Creative Sharing)

Nothing is more important than children encouraged. And children are happiest when they have opportunities to express themselves and to see others doing the same. Through having their creativity recognized and through the realization that everyone else is unique in their expressions, children come to integrate, respect, recognize and appreciate the creations of others. And through this whole process, our children come to accept the responsibility of maintaining a universal freedom of creative potential. With such assimilated values, they then are able to nurture a climate where it is deemed essential for creativity to flourish. And from that wondrous stance, their world - as well as that of their children and grand-children - will be inspired by the one thing now lacking in our time - awe for creative potential. Can we as parents assure less for our own and the world's children?

And so, after my long-winded essay, do I have anything more to add? Only one thing. . .

Children are not beings who are "becoming" anything. They already are. As individuals they already are unique. Children simply live their "process", evolving from birth beginnings and experiences through to their teens and middle life and eventually to just as exciting elder adventures. This is the position of us all. We begin as dependent beings in need of mentoring. And we fulfill our mandate by eventually mentoring those who come after us.

The goal is to maintain our own high level of creative output and to encourage that of ALL children. For the one crucial aspect of creativity which must never be forgotten is that it is not a privilege of the few but rather the one element of life which is universally available to each and every child - when and if that environment *encourages* it.

To all, I say Godspeed on this, our wondrous quest.

# Bibliography

(Alphabetical listing)

**A New Approach To Discipline: Logical Consequences** - Dreikurs, Rudolph M.D. and Grey, Loren

**Behavior, health and environmental stress** - Cohen, S. Evans, G.W. - 1986

**Centuries of Childhood,** (A Social History of Family Life) - Ariès, Philippe - 1962

**Child development and the physical environment**. Annual Review of Psychology - G. W. Evans, 2006

**Childhood** - Konner Melvin

**Children: The Challenge** - Dreikurs, Rudolph M.D. and Soltz, Vicki R.N. - 1964

**Dark Age Ahead -** Jane Jacobs - 2004

**Encouraging Children To Learn** - Dinkmeyer Don PHD and Dreikurs Rudolf MD -

**Education and Income** - Cayo Sexton, Patricia - 1961

**Environmental stress** - Evans, G.W. 1982

**For Your Own Good** - Miller Alice

**Free Range Kids** - Lenore Skenazy, 2009

Il était une fois l'enfant - Chabanis Christian

**La nouvelle ignorance,** (et le problème de la culture) -Thomas De Koninck - 2000

**L'enfant et la vie familiale sous l'Ancien Régime** - Ariès Philippe - 1973

**Man Child**, (A Study Of The Infantilization Of Man) - Jonas David and Klein Doris

**Rock A Bye Baby,** A 1970 Time Life Documentary, (28 min.) Executive Producer: Lothar Wolff

**So Little For The Mind** - Neatby Hilda - 1953

**The Challenge of Child Training**, (A parent's guide) - Dreikurs, Rudolph M.D. - 1972

**The courage to Create** - Rollo May - 1975

**The Creative Habit** - Tharp Twyla

**The Drama Of The Gifted Child** - Miller Alice

**The Dynamics of Creativity** - Anthony Storr

**The environment of poverty**, (Multiple stressor exposure, psychophysiological stress, and socioemotional adjustment. Child Development) - Evans, G.W. & English, K. (2002).

**The Feminized Male** - Cayo Sexton, Patricia - 1969

**The Myth of the Hyperactive Child,** (And Other Means Of Child Control) - Schrag, Peter and Divoky Diane - (1971 - 1976)

**The School of Genius** - Anthony Storr - 1988

**The Untouched Key** - Miller Alice

**Think** - LeGault Michael - 2006

**What Is Creativity? Creativity Explained** - Sylvia Hartmann

**Get Back Up, Nick Vujicic** - YouTube - visual essay on "to fail or not to fail".

# Biography

## Bernard Aimé. Poulin, cipa

For the past 40 years Bernard Poulin has enjoyed a successful international career creating corporate and private portraits as well as commissioned art exhibitions. A Fellow of the Canadian Institute of Portrait Artists he was its President for the 2003-2005 term. Over the years, the internationally prominent figures he has painted are from the political, religious, sport and royal arenas of the world.

A sculptor of bronze (using the lost wax process), Poulin is also a muralist with several three-dimensional, mixed-media projects to his credit. A respected exhibition judge, the author lectures internationally. He has participated in the creation of more than 20 books dedicated to the process of drawing. His articles and television appearances have been translated into Portuguese and Italian. The author of 8 of his own books, the artist is now completing 5 more manuscripts.

Prior to his career in the visual arts, Bernard worked in special education and guest lectured in several colleges, the University of Ottawa and Laurentian University in Sudbury, Ontario Canada.

**For more information please visit at the following address
www.poulinstudios.com**

www.ingramcontent.com/pod-product-compliance
Lightning Source LLC
Chambersburg PA
CBHW022357040426
42450CB00005B/225